# Fruit& Nut
## RECIPES

# 300 easy to prepare recipes using fruit and nuts.

By Dr. Duane R. Lund

Lund S&R Publications

*Distributed by*
Adventure Publications
820 Cleveland
Cambridge, MN 55008

ISBN-10: 0-9740821-3-9
ISBN-13: 978-0-9740821-3-4

1

# Fruit & Nut Recipes

First Printing, 2005
Second Printing, 2006

Printed in the United States of America
by
**Lund S&R Publications**
Staples, Minnesota 56479

*Dedication: to Greg Johnson, my long-time friend and hunting and fishing associate. This book was his idea.*

# TABLE OF CONTENTS

# CHAPTER I
## SMOOTHIES AND OTHER BLENDER RECIPES

# CHAPTER II
## BREAKFASTS USING FRUIT AND/OR NUTS

# CHAPTER III

## PUNCH RECIPES

## CHILLED PUNCH RECIPES

# CHAPTER IV
## HORS D'OEUVRES

## DIPPING SAUCES FOR FRUIT

# CHAPTER V
## SALAD RECIPES

# CHAPTER VI
## FRUITS AND NUTS WITH MEATS

## USING FRUIT AND/OR NUTS IN DRESSING (STUFFING)

## MARINADES

# CHAPTER VII
## FRUIT AND/OR NUTS WITH FISH

# CHAPTER VIII
## FRUIT SALSAS WITH FISH OR GAME

# CHAPTER IX

## WILD FRUITS AND BERRIES

# CHAPTER X

## JUST NUTS

# CHAPTER XI

## FRUIT AND NUTS USED IN BAKING

# CHAPTER XII

## DESSERTS

# CHAPTER I

# SMOOTHIES & OTHER BLENDER RECIPES

# The Crocker Family's Favorite Smoothies*

Crushed ice may be added to any of the recipes to make them colder. Unless otherwise noted, put all ingredients in a blender and blend until smooth.

## Favorite #1

Ingredients:
  2 bananas
  2 mangos (peeled and diced)
  2 cups yogurt or vanilla ice cream
  2 cups orange juice or pineapple juice
  ¼ cup sugar (optional)

## Favorite #2

Ingredients:
  2 bananas
  2 cups strawberries (fresh)
  2 cups vanilla yogurt or vanilla ice cream
  2 cups crushed ice
  ¼ cup sugar (optional)

## Favorite #3

Ingredients:
  2 bananas
  2 peaches (need not be peeled)
  2 nectarines (need not be peeled)
  2 mangos (peeled and diced)
  2 cups vanilla yogurt or ice cream
  3 cups orange juice or pineapple juice
  ½ cup sugar (optional)

# Favorite #4

**Ingredients:**
  2 bananas
  2 cusp fresh strawberries
  2 cups blueberries
  1 cup vanilla yogurt or ice cream
  2 T lemon juice
  ¼ cup sugar (optional)

*Courtesy Kevin, Connie, Hannah, Andrew and Olivia Crocker, Big Lake, Minnesota

# Peach-Banana Smoothie

**Ingredients:**
  1 large can Peaches with juice
  3 bananas, chunked
  2 cups orange juice
  2 cups lemonade
  1 can crushed pineapple, with juice
  9 ice cubes

# Banana Fruit Shake without Milk

**Ingredients to serve 2:**
  2 bananas, peeled and chunked
  3 T honey
  1 cup strawberries or blueberries
  1 cup pineapple juice

Chill all ingredients before blending. Banana chunks may be frozen.

# Banana Cooler

**Ingredients for 1 quart:**
  4 ripe bananas
  1 – 12 oz. can frozen pink lemonade
  1 can water
  12 ice cubes, crushed

# Yogurt-Fruit Smoothie

**Ingredients to serve 4:**
  2 cups plain yogurt (unflavored)
  2 cups skim milk
  2 bananas, peeled, chunked and frozen
  2 cups fresh berries of your choice (strawberries, blueberries or
    raspberries)

# Strawberry-Banana-Orange Smoothies

**Ingredients to serve 2:**
  2 bananas, peeled, chunked and frozen
  1 cup fresh strawberries
  1 cup orange juice, chilled
  1 cup skim milk, chilled

# South Seas Fruit Smoothie

**Ingredients to serve 2:**
  1 mango, chunked
  1 banana, peeled, chunked and frozen
  ½ cup frozen strawberries
  4 T piña colada mix, frozen
  1-½ cups skim milk
  8 ice cubes

# Pear and Banana Smoothie

**Ingredients to serve 2:**
  1 pear, peeled, cored and chunked (or sliced)
  1 banana, peeled, chunked and frozen
  ½ cup frozen berries of your choice
  ¼ T cinnamon
  2 cups skim milk

# Peach-Pineapple-Strawberry Smoothie

**Ingredients to serve 2:**
  ½ cup crushed pineapple, chilled
  1 cup strawberries, frozen
  1 banana, peeled, chunked and frozen
  2 cups skim milk, chilled

# Orange-Ice Cream Smoothie

**Ingredients to serve 4:**
  4 cups orange juice, frozen
  4 large scoops vanilla ice cream
  1 large orange, peeled, seeded and broken into sections
  1 small jar maraschino cherries, including juice

# Fruit Banquet

**Ingredients to serve 4:**
  1 apple, peeled, cored and sliced
  1 cup strawberries
  1 avocado, peeled, cored and diced
  1 orange, peeled, seeded and broken into sections
  1 can pineapple (save juice)
  ½ cup raisins
  2 bananas, sliced
  1 cup shredded coconut

Blend orange, raisins, bananas with pineapple juice.
Pour liquid over fruit and gently stir until well coated. Serve topped with shredded coconut.


## Fruit Soup with Vegetables, Chilled

**Ingredients to serve 4:**
  1 apple, peeled, cored and sliced
  1 orange, peeled, seeded and broken into sections
  1 grapefruit, peeled, seeded and broken into sections
  1 tomato, chunked
  1 stalk celery, chopped
  1 cucumber, peeled, seeded and chunked

Chill all ingredients and then blend until smooth.


## Melon Special with Blended Dressing

**Ingredients to serve 4:**
  ¼ watermelon, balled
  1 cantaloupe, balled
  1 honeydew melon, balled
  1 cup seedless green grapes

**Ingredients for dressing:**
  2 cups pineapple juice
  3 T honey
  1 banana

Blend dressing ingredients and pour over melon balls and grapes, stirring gently to coat.

## Peachy Orange Blend

**Ingredients to serve 4:**
 2 cups orange juice concentrate
 2 cups chunked peaches
 ⅓ cup sugar
 2 cups water
 2 cups ice cubes

Blend first four ingredients. Add ice cubs. Blend until smooth.

## Orange-Banana-Strawberry Blend

**Ingredients to serve 4:**
 2 bananas, chunked
 1 cup strawberries, frozen or fresh
 2 cups orange juice concentrate
 4 T sugar
 2 cups water
 2 cups ice cubes

Blend the first five ingredients. Add ice cubes. Blend until smooth.

# BLENDER RECIPES FOR FRUIT SALADS DRESSINGS

## Recipe #1

**Ingredients for salad for 4:**
 1 avocado, peeled and diced
 4 T frozen pineapple concentrate
 1 banana, chunked
 ½ cup water

Blend all ingredients and pour over fruit of your choosing.

# Recipe #2

**Ingredients for fruit salad for 4:**
  1 banana, chunked
  2 avocados, peeled and diced
  ½ cup frozen orange concentrate
  ⅓ cup water

Blend all ingredients and pour over fruit of your choosing.

# CHAPTER II

# BREAKFASTS

# Introduction

Check out the chapters on Blender Recipes and Wild Fruit and Nuts for other breakfast ideas. There are also fruit juice ideas at the end of the chapter on Punch Recipes.

The berry sauce recipes found in the chapter on Wild Berries and Nuts make a good substitute for syrup or may be combined with syrup for both pancakes and waffles.

## Pancakes and Waffles with Nuts

Use your favorite pancake or waffle recipes and then add pecans or walnuts. You may chop the nuts and mix them into the batter or sprinkle them on top, whole or chopped, as they are served. For a slightly more "nutty" flavor, toast the nuts in a Teflon skillet in light oil for two or three minutes.

## Pancakes or Waffles from Scratch with Nuts #1

**Ingredients for 3 waffles or 6 pancakes:**
   1 cup flour
   1 t baking powder
   1 cup milk for waffles, 1-½ cups for pancakes
   2 eggs
   1 t vanilla extract
   ¼ cup chopped nuts of your choosing

You may use the same recipe for waffles as for pancakes but there is one important difference, waffle batter should be thicker, so use more flour or less milk.

# Waffles or Pancakes from Scratch with Nuts #2

**Ingredients to serve 4:**
  1-¼  cups flour
  1 t baking powder
  3 T brown sugar
  1 cups milk for waffles, 1-½  cups for pancakes
  2 eggs
  dash of salt
  1 t vanilla extract
  3 T melted butter
  ¾ cup chopped pecans or walnuts (not too fine)

The amount of milk you use for pancakes depends on how thick you want them (less milk for thicker pancakes). The batter should be thicker for waffles.

While the waffle iron or pancake griddle is getting hot, toast the nuts two or three minutes in a skillet with a little oil.

Combine the dry ingredients and the wet ingredients separately, then stir the milk-vanilla-egg mixture slowly into the dry ingredients.

The waffles will be done when the iron light goes on or when it stops steaming. For pancakes, check after 2 minutes, turn when bottom side is done.


# Crepes with Nuts

**Ingredients to serve 4:**
  Complete pancake mix or your favorite recipe, baked very thin
  1 cup finely chopped nuts of your choice (walnuts work well)
  4 T rum
  ½ cup sugar
  2 cups milk

Toast the nuts briefly in the oven or in a skillet, then chop fine.

Combine the nuts, sugar and milk. Stir over low-medium heat until sugar dissolves. Add the rum. Set aside.

Prepare 16 to 20 very thin crepes (pancakes) about 6 inches in diameter. Spread the nut-milk-sugar-rum mixture over each crepe and roll into cylinders.

Serve with chocolate or maple syrup.

## Chocolate-Raspberry French Toast

**Ingredients to serve 4:**
   8 slices day-old bread
   4 cups raspberry sauce
   8 T semi-sweet or bitter-sweet chocolate chips
   4 eggs
   8 T complete pancake mix
   2 cups milk (or water)
   1 T vanilla extract
   vegetable oil

Beat the eggs, pancake mix and vanilla extract into the milk or water.
Add a generous amount of cooking oil to a large skillet (pre-heat).
Dip one slice of bread into the egg-milk-pancake mix and transfer to the
skillet. Sprinkle 2 T chocolate chips on top. Dip a second piece of
bread and place on top of the first – like a sandwich. Fry the top and
bottom of each sandwich.
Repeat with the other 6 slices of bread, making three more chocolate
chop sandwiches.
Flip each sandwich over when the bottoms are a golden brown. Fry the
second side of each until brown and the chips have melted.
Pour a cup of raspberry sauce over each sandwich as it is served. Syrup
is optional.


## French Toast with Berries

Prepare and egg wash, using one egg for every two pieces of bread; use
either water or milk. Mix blueberries or strawberries (one cup for four
pieces of bread) into the egg wash.
Use bread that is at least one day old.
As you dip the bread into the egg wash, some berries will stick to the
bread but you many have to spoon additional berries onto the bread
after it is in the skillet. Use a generous amount of oil.

# Over-Night Gourmet French Toast with Chopped Nuts

**Ingredients to serve 4:**
  8 slices of bread, ¾ inch thick (homemade works really well)
  6 eggs
  1-½ cups milk
  2 T sugar
  ½ t salt
  ½ cup vegetable oil
  1 cup chopped walnuts or pecans (toasted)

The night before, combine the eggs, milk, sugar and salt, beat thoroughly.
Arrange the bread in a cake pan in a single layer. Pour the egg-milk mixture over all. Cover and refrigerate over night.
In the morning, fry the bread on both sides in a skillet with a generous amount of oil.
Serve with warm syrup, scatter the chopped nuts over each slice.


# Citrus Breakfast Treat

**Ingredients:**
Enough orange and grapefruit sections to fill a custard cup for each person
3 T melted butter and 2 T brown sugar for each cup

Dissolve the brown sugar in the butter and sprinkle over the fruit in each cup.
Be sure the cups are oven proof! Place them under the broiler for three or four minutes until the liquid is bubbly. Serve warm.

# Fruit Soup

A Scandinavian breakfast treat.

**Ingredients to serve 8-10:**
   2 quarts water
   ½ cup raisins
   1 cup prunes, sliced
   1 cup apricots, sliced (or peaches or other fruit)
   juice of ½ orange
   juice of ½ lemon
   ½ cup sugar
   ½ cup tapioca
   ½ t salt
   1 stick cinnamon

Place the fruit in the water; bring to a boil and then reduce heat and let simmer about 20 minutes. Let cool. Add all other ingredients and cook until the tapioca is transparent. Serve hot or cold.

# Broiled Citrus

**Ingredients to serve 4:**
   Sections of two grapefruit
   Sections of two oranges
   Sections of two tangerines or clementines
   1 cup pineapple chunks
   4 T brown sugar

Using four oven-save custard cups, divide the ingredients equally and sprinkle each with 1 T brown sugar.
Place under the broiler for about 5 minutes or until sugar melts.
Serve warm.

## Wine Enhanced Breakfast Citrus

Ingredients to serve 4:
   Sections of four grapefruit or six oranges or eight tangerines or
      clementines (or combinations thereof)
   ½ cup sweet wine (if not handy, other wines will do, but add more
      sugar)
   ½ cup brown sugar
   2 egg yolks, beaten

Combine the wine, brown sugar and egg yolks, thoroughly. Arrange citrus
sections in four custard or other oven-proof dishes and spoon one
fourth of the mixture over each. Place under a broiler for a few minutes until
ingredients brown, but not burn. Serve warm.

# BREAKFAST JUICES

## Apple-Orange

Ingredients for 3 servings:
   1 cup orange juice
   1 cup apple juice
   1 cup gingerale

Chill before mixing

## Apple-Strawberry-Orange

Ingredients for each serving:
   2 apples, peeled, cored and diced
   2 cups fresh strawberries
   2 oranges, peeled and broken into sections

Process in a juicer, chill and serve.

# Apple-Peach-Pear

**Ingredients for each serving:**
  2 apples, cored and diced
  2 peaches, pitted and diced
  2 pears, cored and sliced

Process through a juicer.


# Orange-Grapefruit

**Ingredients for each serving:**
  Sections of one orange
  Sections of one grapefruit
  1 t lemon juice

Process through a juicer; serve chilled.


# Strawberries-Orange-Lemon

**Ingredients to serve 8:**
  1 pkg. frozen strawberries
  1 can frozen lemonade
  1 can frozen orange juice
  1 liter gingerale (chilled)

Stir ingredients together until frozen ingredients thaw.


# Cranberry-Orange

**Ingredients to serve 4:**
  2 glasses chilled cranberry juice
  2 glasses chilled orange juice

Combine juices in a pitcher, stir together and serve.

# CHAPTER III

# PUNCH RECIPES

# CHILLED PUNCH RECIPES

## Pacific Islands Punch

**Ingredients for about 1-½ gallons:**
   1 cup lemon juice
   ½ cup lime juice
   1-½ cups sugar (or to taste)
   2-½ cups orange juice
   1 – 46 oz. can pineapple juice
   2 liters (one bottle) lemon-lime (carbonated)
   2 liters (one bottle) gingerale
   1 – 10 oz. bottle maraschino cherries

Chill all ingredients in advance.
Freeze each maraschino cherry in an ice cube (save the juice).
In a punch bowl, combine the lemon, orange and lime juices with the
sugar and stir until the sugar is dissolved. Add the pineapple and cherry
juices and stir well. Add the carbonated beverages, pouring slowly
down the inside of the bowl. Stir gently and briefly. Add the ice cubes.
Float a few lemon, lime or orange slices on the surface of the punch.

## Raspberry Sherbet Sparkle

**Ingredients for about 3 quarts:**
   1 cup mint leaves or ⅓ cup dried mint
   ¾ cup sugar
   2 cups boiling water
   2 pkgs. (10 oz. each) frozen raspberries
   2 cans (6 oz. each) frozen lemonade
   4 cans (12 oz. each) carbonated water (raspberry flavored if available)
   1 quart raspberry sherbet

In a saucepan, heat 2 cups of water to boiling. Remove from heat. Add
sugar and mint. Stir. Let stand 10 minutes. Add raspberries and lemonade
concentrate. Stir together. Strain through a sieve. Discard solids. Chill
liquid in refrigerator at least 1 hour.
Pour liquid from above into punch bowl. Add carbonated water, slowly,
along the inside of the bowl. Float small scoops of sherbet in the
punch. If punch will not be consumed immediately, add ice cubes.

# Cranberry Orange Fizz

**Ingredients for about 1 gallon:**
  2 quarts cranberry cocktail juice
  3 cans frozen orange juice concentrate
  1 liter lemon-lime, carbonated (½ bottle)

Chill all liquid ingredients.
In a punch bowl, combine the cranberry cocktail juice and the orange juice concentrate. Stir until the frozen juice dissolves.
Add the carbonated beverage, pouring slowly along the inside of the bowl. Float ice cubes (2 trays) or an ice ring and thin orange slices.


# Lime and Apple Punch

**Ingredients for about 2 quarts:**
  2 cans (6 oz. each) frozen limeade concentrate
  1 quart apple juice
  ½ cup sugar
  ½ t ginger (powdered)
  1 t cinnamon (ground)
  1 quart lemon-lime soda

Chill the apple juice and soda.
In a punch bowl, dissolve the limeade concentrate in the apple juice. Stir in the sugar and spices. Pour in soda, slowly along inside of bowl. Add ice. A nice touch is an ice ring containing fresh strawberries.


# Strawberry Ice Cream and 7-Up Punch

**Ingredients for about 1-½ gallons:**
  6 liters (3 bottles) 7-Up – chilled
  2 quarts strawberry ice cream, brick style
  6 oz. strawberry syrup (ice cream topping)

You may put the bricks of ice cream whole into the punch bowl or cut the bricks up into smaller cubes.

Add the 7-Up, slowly, pouring down the inside of the bowl.

Pour the strawberry syrup "at random" over the ice cream and 7-Up.

Stir very gently (so it doesn't foam up too much).

As it is served, be sure to get some ice cream into each cup.

If you believe it will take awhile to consume the punch, add a tray or two of ice cubes.

## Peach-Citrus-Pineapple Punch with Lime Sherbet

**Ingredients for about 1-½ gallons:**
   2 frozen cans (6 oz.) peach (or apricot) concentrate
   2 frozen cans (6 oz.) pineapple juice concentrate
   2 frozen cans (6 oz.) lemon or limeade concentrate
   3 liters gingerale (1-½ bottles)
   1 quart lime sherbet

Chill the gingerale.

In a punch bowl, dissolve the frozen concentrate in the contents of 1 liter of gingerale. Add the other 2 liters of gingerale, pouring slowly down the inside of the bowl.

Float scoops of sherbet in the punch.

If all of the punch will not be served immediately, add a tray or two of ice cubes.

## Orange-Lemon Punch with Pineapple Sherbet

**Ingredients for about 1-½ gallons:**
   2 cans (6 oz.) frozen orange juice concentrate
   2 cans (6 oz.) frozen lemonade concentrate
   2 cans (6 oz.) frozen pineapple juice concentrate
   4 liters lemon-lime soda (2 bottles)
   3 pints pineapple sherbet

Dissolve the concentrates in 1 of the bottles of lemon-lime soda in a punch bowl. Break the sherbet in pieces and add to the punch. Using a potato masher or large spoon, break the sherbet up until it is "mushy". Add the second bottle of soda, pouring it slowly down the inside of the bowl. If punch will not be consumed immediately, add ice.

## Fruit Juice Punch Flavored with Tea

**Ingredients for about 1 gallon:**
  3 tea bags
  1 cup boiling water
  4 T lemon juice
  1 cup sugar
  1 can (6 oz.) frozen pineapple concentrate
  1 can (6 oz.) frozen orange juice
  1 can (6 oz.) frozen grapefruit juice
  3 liters gingerale (chilled) – (1-½ bottles)

Place tea bags in 1 cup boiling water. Let stand 15 minutes. Discard tea bags. Pour tea into punch bowl, add lemon juice and sugar. Dissolve sugar (some may not dissolve). Add frozen fruit concentrate. Add 1 bottle (1 liter) gingerale and dissolve concentrate. Stir to mix all ingredients and any undissolved sugar. Add another 2 liters of gingerale, pouring slowly down the inside of the bowl. If it tastes too strong for your liking, add more gingerale. Float ice block or cubes. Garnish with thin slices of orange and lemon.
NOTE: This is a different taste than traditional punch recipes. Try it yourself before you serve it to guests! We're quite certain however, that you will really like it.

## Cucumber-Lemon Punch

**Ingredients for about 2 quarts:**
  2 medium cucumbers, peeled, seeded, chopped and pureed.
  2 trays of ice cubes
  2 cans (6 oz.) frozen lemonade concentrate
  3 cans water
  ½ cup sugar
  1 quart (about ½ of a 2 liter bottle) of gingerale

Pre-chill the gingerale.

Place the chopped cucumber in a blender along with a tray of ice cubes. Dissolve the lemon concentrate in the 3 cans of water. Place the cucumber puree, lemonade and sugar in a punch bowl. Pour the gingerale slowly down the inside of the bowl. Add additional ice cubes (second tray). Float thin slices of cucumber as garnish.

## Non-Alcoholic Pina Colada

**Ingredients for about 2 quarts:**
   1 quart pineapple juice, chilled
   1 quart milk, cold
   3 T coconut extract
   2 T vanilla extract
   5 T sugar
   2 trays ice cubes

Using a blender (you may have to make more than one batch, depending on the capacity of your blender). Combine all ingredients at high speed until ice cubes are reduced to slush.

## Quick and Easy Raspberry Punch

**Ingredients for 30 punch-size cups:**
   3 pints raspberry sherbet or ice cream
   3 liters cold gingerale

Let sherbet or ice cream soften, but don't let it melt! Add gingerale slowly to the punch bowl. Optional: Serve with two or three fresh raspberries in each cup.

# Rhubarb-Apple Refresher

**Ingredients for 3 quarts:**
   4 cups fresh rhubarb, cut into small pieces (½ inch)
   water to cover rhubarb in saucepan
   1-½ cups sugar
   1 cup apple cider (or juice)
   1 can (6 oz.) frozen lemonade concentrate
   2 liters (1 bottle) gingerale, chilled

Place the cut-up rhubarb and sugar in a saucepan. Cover with water.
Bring to a boil, then reduce heat to simmer. Continue cooking until
rhubarb is tender. Remove from heat and let cool.
Place cooked rhubarb in a blender and puree. Add cider and lemonade
concentrate and blend thoroughly. (May have to do this in batches).
Place in freezer until ice crystals form. (Do not freeze solid).
Place mixture in a punch bowl, if frozen too hard, break into small
pieces with a spoon. Slowly add the gingerale along the inside of the
bowl.

# Champagne Punch

**Ingredients for about 3 quarts:**
   1 can (6 oz.) pineapple juice concentrate
   1 can (6 oz.) orange juice concentrate
   2 bottles champagne
   1 bottle white wine
   1 can pineapple chunks (drain and save the juice)
   1 pint fresh strawberries

Freeze an ice ring containing the strawberries and pineapple chunks.
Pre-chill the wine and champagne.
In a punch bowl, dissolve the fruit concentrates in the white wine. Add
the champagne, slowly, pouring down the inside of the bowl. Float the
ice ring in the punch.

# Strawberry Sparkle

**Ingredients for about 3 quarts:**
   2 pkgs. frozen strawberries
   2 cans (6 oz.) frozen pink lemonade concentrate, thawed
   3 bottles Catawba grape juice (pink), chilled
   3 cups crushed ice

Mash the thawed strawberries thoroughly. Blend with crushed ice and lemonade concentrate. Place in a punch bowl. Add the Catawba. Blend thoroughly. Be sure some of the crushed strawberries are served in each cup.


# Spicy Sparkle

**Ingredients for about 3 quarts:**
   1 quart cranberry cocktail juice
   1 liter sparkling cider
   1 liter lemon-lime soda or 7-Up

**spicy nectar made from these ingredients:**
   6 cloves
   2 T fresh ginger, chopped fine
   8 inches of cinnamon sticks
   ½ cup sugar
   1 cup water

Prepare the nectar by placing ingredients in a saucepan and bringing to a boil, then reduce heat to simmer. Stir regularly. Remove from heat after 3 or 4 minutes and chill.
Chill the liquids, then combine in a punch bowl. Add the spicy nectar by straining it through a sieve. Stir together, gently. Add ice.

# Raspberry Sparkle

**Ingredients for about 2 quarts:**
  2 pkgs. frozen raspberries
  2 cans frozen limeade
  1 bottle (2 liters) club soda or unflavored carbonated water
  1 pint fresh raspberries
  1 cup vodka (optional)

Freeze fresh raspberries in ice cubes (two trays).
Thaw frozen raspberries and place in punch bowl. Add ½ of the carbonated water. Dissolve frozen limeade. Stir thoroughly. Add vodka (optional) and balance of carbonated water. Float ice cubes.

# Peach-Iced Tea Punch

**Ingredients for approximately 2 quarts:**
  3 cans frozen peach concentrate
  6 cups water
  2 orange pekoe tea bags
  2 T sugar

Heat water in a saucepan to boiling. Pour over tea bags. Let sit 5 minutes. Remove and discard bags. Refrigerate 1 hour.
Place tea in a punch bowl. Stir in sugar. Dissolve frozen peach concentrate in tea.
If punch will not be consumed immediately, float ice cubes to keep cold.

# Banana-Strawberry Punch

**Ingredients for about 2-½ quarts:**
   2 cans (6 oz.) frozen lemonade
   2 cans (6 oz.) frozen orange juice
   2 cans (6 oz.) frozen pineapple juice
   4 ripe bananas
   2 pkgs. frozen strawberries
   4 T sugar
   2 trays ice cubes
   1 bottle (2 liters) 7-Up, chilled
   1 bottle (2 liters) gingerale, chilled

In a blender, combine frozen juices, sugar, bananas, strawberries and ice cubes until "slushy". Add 7-Up and gingerale. (For stronger fruit flavor, add less of the carbonated beverages).


# Cranberry-Pineapple Delight

**Ingredients for about 3 quarts:**
   1 quart cranberry cocktail juice
   2 cans (6 oz.) frozen pineapple juice concentrate
   2 T almond extract
   2 liters (1 bottle) lemon-lime soda

Pre-chill all liquids.
In a punch bowl, combine the cranberry cocktail juice, the pineapple concentrate and the almond extract. Add the lemon-lime soda, pouring slowing down the inside of the bowl.
Add ice cubes or an ice ring containing fresh cranberries and or pineapple chunks.

# Zesty Citrus-Pineapple Punch

**Ingredients for about 1 gallon:**
  2-½ cups sugar
  4 cups water
  4 oranges, juiced
  4 lemons, juiced
  1 can (6 oz.) frozen pineapple juice concentrate
  1 can (6 oz.) frozen peach (or apricot) concentrate
  1 bottle maraschino cherries (save juice)
  2 liters (1 bottle) gingerale

Freeze 1 cherry in each ice cube (about 2 trays).
Pour 4 cups of boiling water over the sugar. Let it dissolve. Add the juice from the oranges and lemons, the cherry juice and the juice concentrates. Refrigerate until well-chilled.
Add the gingerale just before serving, pouring it slowly down the inside of the punch bowl. Float the ice cubes in the punch.


# Cantaloupe Crush

**Ingredients for about 2 quarts:**
  3 cantaloupe, seeded, peeled and diced
  6 T sugar
  1 quart vanilla ice cream
  3 cups crushed or shaved ice

Stir the sugar into the cantaloupe chunks, thoroughly. Place all ingredients in a blender. Puree.


# Cherry-Orange Punch

**Ingredients for about 3 quarts:**
  2 large bottles (10 oz. each) maraschino cherries, save the juice
  1 quart cranberry cocktail juice
  2 cans frozen orange juice concentrate
  water to mix with the orange juice concentrate as directed
  a few drops red food coloring

Freeze 2 trays of ice cubes with a cherry in each cube.
Pre-chill the cherry juice and the cranberry juice cocktail.
Following the directions on the can, reconstitute the orange juice.
Chill.
Combine all ingredients in a punch bowl. Add a few drops of red food coloring until punch is a bright red. Float the ice cubes in the punch.

## Cranberry-Lime Punch

**Ingredients for about 3 quarts:**
   1 quart cranberry juice cocktail, chilled
   2 cans (6 oz.) frozen limeade concentrate
   2 liters (1 bottle) gingerale, chilled

In a punch bowl, dissolve the limeade concentrate in the pre-chilled cranberry juice cocktail. Add the gingerale slowly, pouring down the inside of the bowl. Add ice cubes or an ice block. A nice touch with this punch is an ice ring
containing fresh strawberries (or other fruit).

## Pink Lemonade Punch

**Ingredients for about 2-½ quarts:**
   2 cans (6 oz.) frozen lemonade concentrate
   2 cans water
   1 quart cranberry juice cocktail
   1 quart lemon-lime soda

Refrigerate the cranberry juice cocktail and the soda.
In a punch bowl dissolve the lemonade concentrate in the cranberry juice cocktail, to which two cans of water has been added.
Add the lemon-lime soda slowly, pouring down the inside of the bowl.
Float ice cubes or a block of ice in the punch.

# Creamy Fruit Punch

**Ingredients for 1-½ quarts:**
  1 pint vanilla ice cream
  2 ripe bananas
  1 cup frozen strawberries
  1 cup pineapple juice, chilled
  1 cup frozen raspberries
  1 cup orange juice, chilled

Combine all ingredients in a blender.

# Tahiti Punch

**Ingredients for 1 quart:**
  2 cups pineapple juice
  1 cup orange juice
  1 – 12 oz. can 7-Up
  3 T cream of coconut
  12 ice cubes, crushed

Combine all ingredients in a blender.

# Spicy Apple Juice Punch

**Ingredients for approximately 2-½ quarts:**
  6 cups apple juice
  6 inches stick cinnamon
  8 whole allspice
  1 t vanilla extract
  1 liter Sprite or similar carbonated beverage (or champagne)

Prepare a cheese cloth spice bag containing cinnamon sticks and allspice. Place apple juice and spice bag in a saucepan. Bring to a boil and then let cool. Discard spice bag. Combine cooled apple juice with carbonated beverage and vanilla extract. Serve over ice. Float apple slices for garnishment.

# Citrus-Strawberry Punch

**Ingredients for about 3 quarts:**
  1 pkg. frozen strawberries
  1 can frozen orange juice (6 oz.)
  1 can frozen lemonade (6 oz.)
  1 quart (32 oz.) raspberry or strawberry flavored carbonated water
  1 liter gingerale
  whole strawberries or orange slices for garnishment

Combine all ingredients in a punch bowl over ice. (Add carbonated beverages last, pouring slowly along side of bowl).


# Eggnog with Orange Juice

**Ingredients for about 1 gallon:**
  7 eggs
  ½ cup sugar
  ½ t ground cloves
  1 t cinnamon
  ¼ t ground ginger
  2 quarts orange juice
  1 quart vanilla ice cream (brick)
  1 quart gingerale
  nutmeg for garnish

Chill all liquids.
Beat eggs, thoroughly, blending in sugar, cloves, cinnamon and ginger. Cut the ice cream into 1 inch square chunks. Add the gingerale slowly, pouring down the inside of the bowl. Stir in the seasoned egg mixture. Sprinkle generously with nutmeg.
**WARNING:** *Because raw eggs may contain salmonella bacteria, this recipe may be injurious to one's health – particularly to the young, the elderly and pregnant women.*

## Quick, Fruity Drinks with Gingerale

Spoon 2 or 3 T's of your favorite berry syrup (like strawberry, raspberry, blueberry or pineapple) into the bottom of a tall glass. Fill with chilled gingerale.
PS: Champagne doesn't taste too bad either!


# HOT PUNCH RECIPES

## Hot Lemonade with Rum

**Ingredients for about 1-½ quarts:**
   Juice of 3 lemons
   1 cup sugar
   5 cups water
   6 whole cloves
   1 cup rum

Place all ingredients except the rum in a saucepan. Bring to a boil. Remove from the heat. Remove the cloves. Stir in the rum. Pour into a punch bowl. Thin lemon slices make an attractive garnish. Serve hot.


## Hot Cranberry Punch #1

**Ingredients for about 3 quarts:**
   2 quarts cranberry juice cocktail
   2 cans (6 oz.) frozen pineapple juice concentrate
   8 cans water
   ½ cup brown sugar

**Ingredients for spice bag:**
   4 – 3 inch sticks of cinnamon
   2 T whole cloves
   4 T whole allspice
   dash of salt

In a large saucepan, dissolve the pineapple concentrate in 6 cans of water. Add the cranberry juice cocktail. Stir in a generous dash of salt and the brown sugar.

Make a "spice bag" of cheesecloth containing the cinnamon, allspice and cloves. Place the spice bag in the saucepan. Bring to a boil, then reduce heat and let simmer 10 minutes. Remove spice bag. Serve hot.

## Hot Cranberry Punch #2

**Ingredients for about 1 gallon:**
   1 gallon cranberry juice cocktail
   3 cups brown sugar
   3 – 3 inch sticks of cinnamon
   2 t whole allspice
   2 t whole cloves

Place the cranberry juice cocktail in the bottom portion of a large coffee percolator. Place the spices and sugar in the basket. Let percolate through the entire cycle. Serve hot.

## Peachy-Pineapple Wassail

**Ingredients for about 2 quarts:**
   2 cans (6 oz.) pineapple juice concentrate
   2 cans (6 oz.) peach (or apricot) frozen concentrate
   6 cans water
   2 cups apple cider
   ½ cup sugar

**Ingredients for the "spice bag":**
   3 – 3 inch sticks cinnamon
   1 t whole cloves
   1 t allspice

In a saucepan, dissolve the fruit concentrate and sugar in 6 cans of water. Make a spice bag of cheese cloth, containing the cinnamon, allspice and cloves. Place the spice bag in the mixture in the saucepan. Bring to a boil, then reduce heat to simmer for 10 minutes. Remove and discard spices. Serve hot.

# Zesty Cider

**Ingredients for about 3 quarts:**
  1 quart apple cider
  1 can (6 oz.) frozen pineapple juice
  1 can (6 oz.) frozen orange concentrate
  4 cans water
  1 liter (half bottle) gingerale (room temperature)
  ¼ cup sugar

**Ingredients for a "spice bag":**
  2 – 3 inch sticks cinnamon
  1 t whole allspice
  1 t whole cloves

In a large saucepan, place the cider, frozen fruit juices, sugar and water. Stir until dissolved. Make a spice bag of cheese cloth containing the 3 spices. Place this in the saucepan. Bring to a boil. Reduce heat to simmer until piping hot, 10-15 minutes. Remove from heat. Remove and discard spices. Pour into a punch bowl. Add gingerale. Serve immediately in warm cups.

# Hot Mulled Cider

**Ingredients for about 1 gallon:**
  1 gallon apple cider
  1 heaping cup brown sugar
  dash of salt

**Ingredients for a "spice bag":**
  2 t whole cloves
  2 – 3 inch cinnamon sticks
  2 t whole allspice

Prepare a spice bag of cheese cloth for the 3 spices. Dissolve the brown sugar in the cider in a saucepan. Add the spice bag. Bring to a boil, then reduce heat to "simmer" for about 15 minutes. Remove and discard the spice bag. Serve immediately in warm cups.

# Quick Hot Mulled Cider

**Ingredients:**
  apple cider
  cinnamon sticks
  orange slices
  whole cloves

Heat the apple cider to boiling point, but do not let boil.
Pre-arrange a cinnamon stick and an orange slice studded with 3 whole cloves in warm cups.
Fill each cup with hot cider. Encourage guests to stir their drink for a minute or so before they enjoy it.

# Hot Apple Cider and Cranberry Juice Cocktail

**Ingredients for about 1 gallon:**
  2 liters apple cider
  2 liters cranberry juice cocktail
  1 cup brown sugar
  3 – 3 inch sticks of cinnamon
  2 t whole allspice
  2 t whole cloves

Place the apple cider and cranberry juice in the bottom of a large coffee percolator. Place all dry ingredients in the basket. Percolate through one complete cycle. Serve hot.

# CHAPTER IV

# HORS D'OEUVRES

## Avocado Spread

Ingredients:
  2 avocados, crushed
  8 oz. cream cheese
  a few drops of Tabasco or other hot sauce to taste

## Hawaiian Spread

Ingredients:
  2 cans (5-½ oz.) crushed pineapple, drained
  8 oz. cream cheese
  ½ cup Macadamia nuts, chopped

Mix thoroughly. For a more "zesty" flavor, add 4 finely chopped green onions, including the greens.

## Crab Meat and Avocado Spread

Ingredients:
  1 cups shredded (or chopped) pre-cooked crab meat (may use artificial)
  1 cup mashed avocado
  4 oz. cream cheese
  4 T mayonnaise

Stir together, thoroughly. For a sharper taste, add a few drips of Tabasco or other hot sauce.

## Nutty Cheese Spread

Ingredients:
  8 oz. grated cheese (cheddar works well)
  ⅔ cup finely chopped nuts (try pecans, almonds or cashews)
  6 slices bacon, fried crisp and chopped
  ¾ cup mayonnaise
  2 t minced onion

Combine all ingredients, thoroughly. Serve on crackers or toast points.

# Stuffed Mushrooms with Chopped Nuts

Ingredients:
  24 large mushrooms
  ¼ cup chopped walnuts (or almonds or cashews)
  ⅛ pound butter
  2 T chives, chopped
  salt, pepper and garlic salt

Remove stems. Cut stems and sauté pieces in butter. Add all other ingredients, seasoning lightly and stuff caps. Arrange in baking dish. Broil until mushrooms are a light brown (usually 5 or 6 minutes). Alternate ingredients: four slices of bacon, broiled and crumbled.


# Water Chestnut-Chicken Liver-Bacon Sandwich

Ingredients for about 24 servings:
  1 can water chestnut halves
  8 chicken livers (more or less depending on size of livers)
  12 strips bacon
  2 cups oil for deep frying

Cut the chicken livers into pieces slightly larger than the water chestnut halves. Make a sandwich with a piece of chicken liver on each side of a chestnut half. Wrap each with a strip of bacon and pin with a toothpick. Pre-heat the oil in the fryer. Carefully float the sandwiches in the oil – only a couple of minutes until the bacon is crisp.


# Woodticks on a Poplar Tree

Ingredients:
  Several ribs of celery cut into 2″ chunks
  1 pkg. cream cheese
  1 cup raisins

Cut and clean the ribs from a stalk of celery and then cut them into chunks about 2 inches long. Fill the indented sides of the celery pieces with cream cheese. Press 4 or 5 raisins into the cheese on each chunk.

# Dates Stuffed with Cheese and Wrapped with Bacon

**Ingredients:**
   24 pitted dates
   1 pkg. (4 oz.) cream cheese
   12 slices thin bacon

Slice the dates open and stuff them with cream cheese.
Meanwhile, broil the bacon strips until they are well done but not
crisp. Cut each slice in half. Wrap each stuffed date with a piece of
bacon and secure it with a toothpick.

# Apple Slices with Cheese

**Ingredients:**
   4 or 5 large, hard, red apples (such as Winesap or Prairie Spy), cored
   and sliced
   16 oz. mild cream cheese
   ½ cup sour cream
   5 T rum or brandy of your choice (optional)
   1 T mustard (Dijon)

Core and slice the apple. Dip each slice in a glass of water in which a
few drops of lemon juice has been dissolved (to prevent discoloring).
Combine all other ingredients.
Spread on apple slices. Serve.

# Stuffed Strawberries

**Ingredients for 36 hors d'oeuvres:**
   3 dozen plump, red strawberries
   4 oz. strawberry flavored cream cheese
   4 T sour cream
   4 T mayonnaise

Combine cream cheese, sour cream and mayo, thoroughly. Remove
stems from berries. Set each berry on end, point up. Starting at the
point of each berry, cut an "X" ⅔ of the way down. Spoon or "pipe" the
mixture into the center of each berry. Stop when the cheese mixture
starts to ooze out of the cuts.

## Apple Dip

**Ingredients:**
   4 apples, peeled, cored and sliced
   4 oz. cream cheese
   4 T brown sugar
   1 T vanilla extract

Combine cheese, brown sugar and vanilla and dip slices of apple.

## Fruit Stuffed with Cheese

**Ingredients:**
   4 oz. blue cheese, crumbled
   4 oz. cream cheese (soften at room temperature)
   1 cup finely chopped walnuts or pecans

Combine all ingredients and stuff fruit such as dates, dried apricots or pears (halved, peeled and cored). Apricots and dates should be cut almost through and opened so they can be stuffed, then partially closed.

# DIPPING SAUCES FOR FRUIT

## Cream with Wine

**Ingredients:**
   ⅔ cup whipping (heavy) cream
   2 T white wine
   3 T powdered sugar

Combine the three ingredients.

## Chocolate-Cherry

**Ingredients:**
   ⅔ cup whipping (heavy) cream
   6 oz. German sweet chocolate, chopped fine
   3 T butter
   3 T cherry brandy

Combine cream, chocolate and butter in a saucepan over low heat; stir until chocolate is melted. Remove from heat and stir in brandy.

## Creamy Almond

Ingredients:
⅔ cup whipping (heavy) cream
6 oz. White chocolate, chopped fine
3 T butter
3 T Amaretto (almond flavor) liqueur (1 T almond extract may be substituted)

Combine cream, chocolate and butter in a saucepan over low heat. Stir until chocolate is melted. Remove from heat and stir in liqueur.

## Sour Cream-Mayo Fruit Dip

Ingredients:
1 can crushed pineapple, including juice
1-½ cups sour cream
1 cup mayonnaise
1-½ cups fruit of your choosing, diced fine

Combine all ingredients and chill.
Use a dip for fruit of your choosing, such as apple slices, orange sections or pear slices.

## Cream Cheese-Marshmallow Dip

Ingredients:
Mix equal portions (by volume) of cream cheese and marshmallow cream.
Most any kind of fruit will go well with this dip.

# CHAPTER V

# SALAD RECIPES

Let's start with a quick and easy one.

## Pineapple and Cottage Cheese Salad

**Ingredients to serve 6:**
    1 small can pineapple slices (save juice)
    6 scoops cottage cheese
    Maraschino cherries (small jar) discard juice
    French or Russian dressing

Place one pineapple ring on each salad plate. Top with a scoop of cottage cheese. Drizzle the pineapple juice over the cottage cheese. Top cottage cheese with one or two cherries. Pour liberal portions of French or Russian dressing over all.

## Fruit and Nut Salad

**Ingredients to serve 4:**
    1 pear, peeled, cored and sliced or chunked
    1 apple, peeled, cored and sliced or chunked
    1 orange or 2 tangerines, broken into sections
    ⅔ cup chopped walnuts (or other nuts of your liking)
    lettuce leaves
    salad oil of your choosing, or mix together equal portions of
    vegetable oil, honey and white wine (or wine vinegar)

Make a bed of lettuce leaves on each plate. Mix fruit and nuts and spoon onto each plate. Drizzle oil mixture over each salad.

## Maple Flavored Mango and Berry Salad

**Ingredients to serve 6:**
    2 mangos, peeled and chunked
    3 cups blueberries (or other favorite berry)
    6 T maple syrup
    lettuce leaves

Make a bed of lettuce on each salad plate.
Gently combine fruit. Add syrup and stir together thoroughly but carefully. Spoon onto the beds of lettuce.
This may be served as a desert in shallow bowls, but skip the lettuce.

## Blueberry and Banana Salad

**Ingredients to serve 4:**
   2 bananas, peeled and sliced
   1-½ cups blueberries
   2 tangerines, broken into sections (may substitute 1 large orange or canned Mandarin oranges)
   1 cup yogurt (plain or berry flavored)
   4 T shredded coconut

Combine fruit. Gently fold in the yogurt. Spoon equal portions on four salad plates. Top with shredded coconut.

## Fruit with Fruit Juice Dressing

**Ingredients to serve 6:**
   2 bananas, peeled and sliced
   1 apple, peeled, cored and sliced
   1 pear, peeled, cored and sliced
   1 can pineapple in chunks (save the juice)
   1 pkg. regular (not instant) vanilla pudding
   1-½ cups orange juice

Prepare and mix fruit and chill.
Meanwhile, place orange juice, pudding mix and pineapple juice in a saucepan. Heat and stir until it starts to thicken. Stir the dressing into the fruit mixture and return to refrigerator for at least 1 hour to chill.

# Zesty Fruit Salad

**Ingredients to serve 6:**
 1 large can pineapple chunks (save juice)
 3 tangerines, peeled and broken into sections
 1-½ cups strawberries
 1 cup blueberries
 1 cup white zinfandel wine
 1 cup 7-Up

Combine fruit in a large bowl. Combine the pineapple juice, wine and 7-Up. Gently stir in the liquid. Refrigerate 2 hours, stirring at least twice and once more before serving. Place equal portions of fruit on salad plates, using a
slotted spoon. Drizzle liquid remaining in the bowl over each serving.

# Grape and Walnut Salad

**Ingredients to serve 4:**
 2 cups seedless grapes, halved
 1 cup whipped cream
 8 oz. cream cheese
 ⅔ cup chopped walnuts

Blend together the whipped cream and cream cheese. Blend in the walnuts. Blend in the grapes. Chill (no more than 1 hour) and serve.

# Kathy's Fruit Salad with Poppy Seed Dressing*

**Ingredients to serve 4:**
 1 bag Romaine lettuce
 1 handful shredded Swiss cheese
 1 handful cashews
 ¼ cup dried cranberries
 ½ apple, chopped fine
 ½ pear, chopped fine
 (drizzle apple and pear with lemon juice)

**Ingredients for dressing (in blender)**
 ½ cup sugar
 ⅓ cup lemon juice
 2 t chopped onion
 ½ t salt

Blend, and then stir in 1 T poppy seeds and 2/3 cup oil.
Drizzle over salad and serve.

*Courtesy Kathy Miller, Grand Rapids, MN

# Fruit Enhancement

**Prepare a sauce by combining:**
 1 can lemon-lime soda
 ½ cup sugar
 2 T cornstarch
 fruit of your choosing (may be a variety)

Bring the first 3 ingredients to a boil in a saucepan. Reduce heat and
let simmer, stirring until sauce starts to thicken (about 2 minutes).
Refrigerate until cold.
Use the fruit of your choice, such as seedless grapes, sections of
oranges, sections of grapefruit, blueberries, strawberries, etc.
Combine the variety of fruit you have chosen. Coat by stirring in the
sauce.

# Spinach Salad with Strawberries

Use your favorite spinach salad recipe and just add the strawberries or
use this one:

**Ingredients to serve 4:**
 4 cups spinach leaves, torn
 2 cups frozen strawberries, thawed (or fresh, halved)
 3 T sugar
 1 T sesame seeds
 3 T wine vinegar
 ¼ t garlic powder
 ⅓ cup salad oil of your choosing

Combine the spinach leaves, strawberries and sesame seeds. Shake together the oil, garlic powder, vinegar and sugar.
Mix all ingredients together thoroughly and then distribute into the salad bowls.

## South Seas Fruit Salad

**Ingredients to serve 6:**
    2 mangos, chunked
    2 oranges, peeled and broken into sections (or tangerines)
    2 papayas, chunked
    1 banana, sliced
    1 small can pineapple chunks (save juice)
    ½ cup coconut cream

**Dressing:**
    1 banana
    4 T citrus fruit marmalade
    1 cup orange juice
    pineapple juice saved from the can

Blend the dressing ingredients (in a blender) until smooth.
Gently combine the dressing and coconut cream with the fruit ingredients and distribute into salad bowls.

## Melon Ball Salad

**Ingredients to serve 4:**
    6 cups assorted melon balls (watermelon, cantaloupe and/or honeydew)
    1 cup seedless grapes (halved)

Use your favorite fruit salad dressing or combine 1 cup white wine with 1 cup gingerale or 7-Up.

# Fruit Basket Upset

**Ingredients to serve 6:**
  1 banana, sliced
  1 orange, peeled and broken into sections
  1 mango, chunked
  1 avocado, sliced
  1 papaya, chunked
  ½ cup shredded coconut

Combine the fruit and prepare a dressing (using a blender) from:

  2 bananas
  ½ cup raisins or pitted dates
  1 small can pineapple chunks, including juice

Blend until smooth. Then gently stir dressing into fruit. Spoon portions into salad bowls. Sprinkle shredded coconut over each serving.


# Melon Balls with a Variety of Fruit

**Ingredients to serve 8:**
  2 cups watermelon balls
  2 cups cantaloupe balls
  2 bananas, sliced
  1 mango, chunked
  1 apple, peeled, cored and sliced
  1 pear, cored, peeled and sliced or chunked
  2 tangerines, peeled and broken into sections

Combine all fruit ingredients in a large bowl and then, using a blender, prepare a dressing from the following:

  4 T blueberry or strawberry jam
  2 bananas, chunked
  2 oranges, peeled and broken into sections
  1 cup of pineapple juice (or any other fruit juice you have on hand)

Blend until smooth, and then gently stir into the bowl of fruit.

# "Whatever Fruit is Handy" Salad

Test your creativity!

Peel and slice (or chunk) whatever fruit you have in the house, like apples, oranges, bananas, grapes, melons, avocados, etc.
Prepare a dressing in a blender of raisins or pitted dates and whatever fruit juices you have on hand.
If you have shredded coconut in the house, top the salad servings with that. Have fun!

# Nutty Fruit Salad

**Ingredients to serve 4:**
   1 pear, peeled, seeded and diced
   1 peach, peeled, seeded and diced
   1 apple, peeled, seeded and diced
   1 cup seedless grapes, halved
   1 cup yogurt
   2 T lime juice
   ⅔ cup of your favorite nuts, chopped (not too fine)

Gently blend together all ingredients and serve. Hint: It will taste even better if you refrigerate at least 30 minutes and the nuts are toasted.

# Plan-Ahead Jell-O Salad

**Ingredients to serve 8:**
   2 pkgs. strawberry Jell-O
   2 cups boiling water
   2 cups cold water
   1 pkg. frozen strawberries, thawed
   3 bananas, sliced
   2 cups miniature marshmallows
   1 pkg. cream cheese
   whipped cream (1-½ cups)

Dissolve Jell-O powder in boiling water in a bowl. Add cold water, bananas and about ⅔ of the strawberries and marshmallows. Pour into a square or
rectangular dish or pan (about 8″x10″) greased with cooking oil or non-stick spray. Refrigerate until firm. Spread softened cream cheese over contents of the pan. Layer on a generous portion of whipped cream. Scatter the remaining strawberries on top and cut into serving size squares.


## Plan-Ahead Cranberry Salad

**Ingredients to serve 6:**
   2 cups cranberries (frozen, fresh or in sauce)
   ½ cup sugar
   2 cups miniature marshmallows
   ½ cup seedless grapes, halved
   ½ cup walnuts, chopped
   1 cup whipped cream
   lettuce leaves

Chop cranberries in a blender. Stir in sugar and marshmallows. Refrigerate overnight (or at least 3 hours). Stir in grapes, nuts and whipped cream just before serving. Serve on a lettuce leaf.


## Mandarin Orange Salad*

**Ingredients to serve 6:**
   Enough lettuce or salad greens to serve 6
   Small can Mandarin orange slices, drained
   1 cup sliced almonds, sautéed in butter until brown
   Paul Newman olive oil and vinegar dressing

Sauté almonds in butter. Gently toss together all ingredients.

*Courtesy Betsy Hayenga, Cushing, MN

# Pear Salad with Walnuts

**Ingredients to serve 4:**
　4 medium sized pears
　⅔ cup chopped walnuts (not too fine)
　enough lettuce to make a bed on each salad plate
　your favorite salad oil

Toast the walnuts in a Teflon skilled in a little oil a couple of minutes, stirring occasionally.
Slice the pears, fairly thin – bite size.
Scatter the pear halves over each plate of lettuce, add the walnuts and sprinkle with salad oil.

# Pear with Cheese Salad

**Ingredients to serve 4:**
　4 large, ripe pears, cored
　8 heaping T's blue cheese, crumbled
　½ cup chopped walnuts (toasted 2 or 3 minutes in dry pan)
　salad dressing of your choice – such as oil and vinegar

Arrange 2 half pears, flat side up, on each saucer.
Place equal portions of crumbled blue cheese in each of the cored, half pears. Sprinkle chopped walnuts over each. Top with dressing.

# My Mother's Fruit Salad

**Ingredients to serve 8:**
　1 cup chopped pecans (lightly toasted)
　2 cans fruit cocktail, drained
　1 medium can pineapple chunks, drained
　2 large oranges or 4 tangerines, peeled and broken into sections
　2 apples, peeled, cored and sliced or chunked
　4 cups miniature marshmallows
　3 cups shredded coconut
　1 small jar maraschino cherries (including juice)
　1 pint whipping cream

Combine all ingredients in a large bowl, and then blend in the whipped cream.

## Apple-Walnut-Blue Cheese Salad

**Ingredients to serve 4:**
  2 large apples, peeled, cored and sliced
  4 cups torn lettuce
  1 cup blue cheese, crumbled
  1 sweet onion, broken into half-rings
  ½ cup olive oil
  2 T mustard
  3 T honey
  1 T sesame seeds
  ⅔ cup chopped walnuts, lightly toasted

Combine olive oil, mustard and honey for dressing. Combine all other ingredients and then carefully blend in the dressing.

## Fruit and Vegetable Salad

**Ingredients to serve 4:**
  2 oranges, peeled and broken into sections
  1 avocado, diced but not fine
  1 cucumber, peeled, seeded and diced
  1 rib celery, chopped
  2 T chopped red pepper
  2 T chopped green pepper
  2 cups lettuce, torn
  ½ cup olive oil
  ½ cup white wine or white wine vinegar

Combine vinegar and oil for a dressing. Combine all ingredients.

## Heavenly Honeydew

**Ingredients to serve 4:**
  2 cups honeydew melon balls (or chunks)
  1 apple, peeled, cored and chunked
  1 cup seedless grapes (halved if they are large)
  2 kiwi fruit, peeled and diced
  1 cup pineapple chunks

Combine all ingredients and blend in your favorite fruit salad dressing or make a dressing of 2 T lime or lemon juice and ½ cup grape juice (white grape juice looks better).

## Mainly Avocado

**Ingredients to serve 6:**
  4 avocados, pitted, peeled and chunked
  1 cup seedless grapes (if they are large, cut them in half)
  2 apples, peeled, cored and chunked
  1 banana, sliced
  1 cup yogurt (plain or citrus flavored)
  2 T honey
  2 T lime juice (or lemon)

Make a dressing of the yogurt, honey and juice. Combine fruit and blend in the dressing.

# Heavy on the Marshmallows!

**Ingredients to serve 6 to 8:**
  1 cup blueberries
  1 pkg. frozen strawberries, thawed
  1 - 16 oz. can Mandarin oranges, drained
  1 small can diced pineapple, drained
  2 dozen large marshmallows, each cut in half
  2 egg yolks
  ½ cup milk
  ⅔ cup whipping cream
  2 t sugar
  ½ t vanilla
  ½ cup chopped nuts (toasted)

Combine fruit and set aside.
Combine the milk and egg yolks, beat thoroughly, heat in a sauce pan (do not boil) for 5 minutes. Let cool, then stir into bowl of marshmallows.
Combine the sugar, cream and vanilla and beat until the whipped cream peaks.
Combine fruit, egg mixture and whipped cream and refrigerate (serve cold).
Sprinkle each serving with chopped nuts.


# Cantaloupe Fruit Bowl

**Ingredients to serve 4:**
  2 cantaloupe, each cut in two and seeds scooped out. (a jagged cut has better eye appeal)
  1 cup strawberries (frozen or fresh cut in halves)
  1 cup blueberries
  1 banana, sliced
  ½ cup green, seedless grapes
  8 t maple syrup

Divide the fruit equally into the cantaloupe halves. Sprinkle each serving with 2 t maple syrup.

# Pecan-Pear Salad

**Ingredients to serve 4:**
   4 cups salad greens
   4 pears, cored and sliced (peel if skin is rough)
   ⅔ cup pecans, chopped and toasted
   oil and vinegar dressing (or your favorite)

Divide salad greens among four plates. Decorate with pear slices and sprinkle with pecans. Let your guests add oil and vinegar. Some may want to add
freshly ground pepper.


# Apple with Bacon Salad

**Ingredients to serve 6:**
   1 head of lettuce broken/torn into bite-size
   2 apples sliced into narrow wedges
   6 slices bacon, broiled until crisp and cut into narrow strips
   12 T (2 per serving) grated cheese of your choosing
   12 T (2 per serving) slivered almonds
   freshly ground pepper

**Dressing ingredients:**
   Use a dressing of your choosing or try this:
   1 cup sour cream
   1 cup light mayonnaise
   4 T catsup (optional)

For a different treatment, sauté the apple slices in butter.

# Apple Coleslaw

**Ingredients to serve 8:**
  6 cups shredded cabbage
  3 apples, peeled, cored and diced
  1 cup green seedless grapes (halved if you have time)
  1 cup chopped sweet pickles
  3 T chopped sweet onion
  1 cup light mayonnaise (or coleslaw dressing)
  3 T sugar
  2 T vinegar
  3 T chopped sweet onion

Combine the cabbage, apples, grapes, pickles and onions. In a smaller bowl, combine the mayo, sugar and vinegar. Stir the contents of the smaller bowl into the contents of the larger bowl.

# Fruit Salad with Poppy Seeds and/or Sesame Seeds and Almonds

**Ingredients to serve 4:**
  1 small can Limeade concentrate
  ½ cup honey
  2 t poppy seeds
  2 t sesame seeds
  4 "heaping" cups of fruit of your choice. A variety works best – such as blueberries, strawberries, watermelon, pineapple, etc.
  ⅓ cup toasted slivered almonds

Combine the limeade concentrate, honey and seeds. In a separate bowl, combine the fruit. Drizzle the liquid mixture over the fruit and carefully stir to coat.

# Fruit, Vegetable and Nut Salad

**Ingredients to serve 6:**
    1 - 16 oz. can Mandarin oranges, drained but save liquid
    1 cup seedless grapes, red or green (halved if you have time)
    2 cups broccoli florets
    2 cups cauliflower florets
    1 cup frozen peas, thawed
    1 rib celery, chopped
    1 cup mayonnaise
    ⅔ cup toasted nuts, chopped (or slivered almonds)

Combine the fruit and vegetables in a large bowl.
Combine the mayonnaise and liquid from the oranges.
Gently stir the mayonnaise-orange juice mixture into the vegetables.
Sprinkle nuts over each serving.


# Chicken Salad

**Ingredients to serve 8:**
    1 quart cooked, diced chicken
    1 small onion, chopped
    2 ribs celery, chopped
    2 oranges, peeled and broken into sections (or 4 tangerines or
       clementines)
    2 small cans crushed pineapple, drained
    3 T chopped green pepper (or red or mixed)
    1 pint light mayonnaise
    2 T prepared mustard
    1 t salt
    2 t black pepper

Combine all ingredients. Chill before serving.

# Oranges and Almonds

**Ingredients to serve 4:**
  4 cups lettuce, torn bite-size
  6 clementine oranges, broken into sections*
  ½ cup chopped celery
  4 slices bacon, broiled crisp and broken into bits
  ½ cup slivered almonds
  oil and vinegar

Combine all ingredients, adding oil and vinegar last.
*oranges or tangerines may be substituted.

# Salad with Grilled Chicken Strips

**Ingredients to serve 6:**
  1 chicken breast (both half-breasts) cut into narrow strips (½ inch)
    and grilled (serve hot)
  6 cups lettuce torn bite-size
  1 tomato, cut into wedges
  2 oranges, peeled and broken into sections
  2 hard-boiled eggs, sliced
  1 pkg. frozen peas, thawed
  4 slices bacon, broiled crisp and cut crossways into narrow strips

Serve with your favorite dressing.

# Fruit Salad with Shrimp

**Ingredients to serve 4:**
  4 cups of assorted fruits, sliced and/or chunked, such as oranges,
    apples, pears, pineapple, etc.
  2 T lemon or lime juice
  2 T chopped onion
  2 T chopped celery
  2 dozen cooked shrimp (tails and veins removed)

Combine and serve with your favorite dressing.

# Spring Garden Salad

**Ingredients to serve 4:**
    4 cups garden lettuce or head lettuce torn bite-size
    4 shallots (green onions) chopped; both white and green parts
    1 cup frozen strawberries, thawed or fresh garden strawberries, halved
       and sugared
    ½ cup slivered almonds
    ground black pepper to taste

Serve with a dressing of your choice or use virgin olive oil and vinegar (raspberry flavored if available).


# Purple Lady Salad*

**Ingredients to serve 6-8:**
    2 – 3 oz. boxes raspberry Jell-O
    1 can blueberry pie filling
    2 cups boiling water
    1 – 8 oz. can crushed pineapple
    8 oz. Cool Whip
    ½ cup chopped pecans

Dissolve Jell-O in boiling water and add pie filling and crushed pineapple with juice.
Cool until it starts to set, then stir in the Cool Whip and chopped pecans.
Refrigerate until completely set.

*Courtesy Judy Droubie, Staples, MN

# South Seas Chicken Salad

**Ingredients to serve 6:**
   2 cups pre-cooked, diced chicken
   2 oranges, peeled and broken into sections
   1 cup seedless grapes (red or green) cut into halves
   2 bananas, sliced
   1 can pineapple tidbits (20 oz.) drained
   3 ribs celery, chopped
   ½ cup cashew halves
   ⅔ cup mayonnaise
   ½ t salt
   ¼ t pepper

Combine all ingredients except bananas and nuts and refrigerate. Add bananas and sprinkle with cashews just before serving.


# South of the Border Fruit Salad

**Ingredients to serve 6:**
   2 cups melon balls (either watermelon or cantaloupe or mixed)
   2 cups fresh pineapple chunks
   2 cups strawberries, halved
   2 cups blueberries
   ½ cup orange juice
   ½ cup pineapple juice (may substitute other fruit juice)
   ½ cup white wine (optional)
   1 t chili powder

Combine all ingredients. Be especially careful to distribute chili powder evenly. Distribute into salad bowls with a slotted spoon and then pour equal amounts of fruit juice over the fruit in each bowl.


# Helen's Romaine, Strawberry and Onion Salad*

**Ingredients to serve 4 or 5:**
   1 bunch Romaine lettuce, torn into bite size pieces
   1 pint sliced strawberries
   ½ medium red onion, chopped

**Ingredients for the dressing:**
¾ cup mayonnaise
2 t poppy seeds
2 T white vinegar
⅓ cup sugar
¼ cup milk

Mix dressing in advance (1 day) for best flavor.
Toss all ingredients together just before serving.

*Courtesy Helen Mennis, Staples, MN

## Judy's Lettuce Salad Exceptionale*

**Ingredients to serve 4 or 5:**
1 head Romaine lettuce, torn into small pieces
½ red onion, slice thin
1 pint fresh strawberries, sliced thin

**Dressing ingredients:**
2 T raspberry vinegar
2 T poppy seed
⅔ cup mayonnaise
⅓ cup sugar

*Courtesy Judy Jenkins, Staples, MN

## Pear Walnut Salad*

**Ingredients to serve 4 or 5:**
4 cups lettuce, torn into pieces
1 pear, sliced (red apple may be used)
⅓ cup toasted walnut halves (toast 3 to 5 minutes at 375 degrees)
2 oz. blue cheese, crumbled

**Dressing ingredients:**
  ½ cup oil
  3 t vinegar
  ¼ cup sugar
  ½ t celery seed
  ¼ t salt

*Courtesy Judy Jenkins, Staples, MN

# Fruity Chicken Salad

**Ingredients to serve 4 to 6:**
  4 cups diced, cooked chicken (bite-size)
  6 cups lettuce, torn into bits
  1 mango, diced
  1 avocado, diced
  1 small can pineapple tidbits (save juice)
  2 green onions, chopped fine (both white and green parts)
  1 cup fresh cilantro, chopped
  3 T lime juice
  ½ cup olive oil

Gently combine all ingredients (including pineapple juice).

# Featuring Apples, Nuts and Blue Cheese

**Ingredients to serve 4 or 5:**
  5 cups Romaine lettuce, torn into bits
  1 tomato, cut into wedges
  1 apple or pear, diced
  1 red onion, broken into circles
  1 avocado, diced
  ⅓ cup pecans, toasted and chopped

**Dressing ingredients:**
  ½ cup blue cheese, crumbled
  ⅓ cup orange juice
  2 T vinegar
  1 T Dijon mustard
  ½ cup mayonnaise
Combine dressing ingredients, and then toss with salad ingredients.

# Fruit Salad with a Ginger-Snap!

**Ingredients for ginger syrup:**
  1 cup water
  1 cup sugar
  1 cup ginger (fresh), sliced thin

Combine the 3 ingredients in a saucepan and bring to a boil; reduce heat and stir until sugar is dissolved and liquid is "syrupy".
Combine 4 cups of mixed fruit, bite size, such as melon, blueberries, strawberries, peaches, pears, etc.
Gently stir in ½ cup of the ginger syrup. Refrigerate the balance for your next fruit salad.

# CHAPTER VI

# FRUIT AND NUTS WITH MEATS

# Diced Ham with Oranges, Pineapple and Almonds

**Ingredients to serve 4:**
  2 pounds cooked ham, diced bite-size
  1 – 16 oz. can diced pineapple, drained
  1 – 16 oz. can Mandarin oranges, drained
  ¼ cup chopped green sweet pepper (bell)
  ¼ cup red sweet pepper (bell)
  1 cup mayonnaise (not fat free)
  ⅓ cup shredded mozzarella cheese
  ½ cup slivered almonds

Combine, carefully, all ingredients except the almonds.
Spoon ingredients into a lubricated baking dish or pan.
Sprinkle almonds over surface.
Bake in a pre-heated 400 degree oven for 30 minutes.

# Ham with Fruit Medley

**Ingredients to serve 4:**
  2 pound cooked ham (four slices)
  1 – 16 oz. can peach halves or slices, save juice
  1 – 16 oz. can pears, sliced, save juice
  1 – 20 oz. can diced pineapple, save juice
  1 small bottle maraschino cherries, drained

Pour the juices saved from the 3 cans into a baking dish or pan large
enough to bake the ham in a single layer. Scatter the fruit over the ham.
Bake in a pre-heated 350 degree oven 30 minutes. Serve the ham
sprinkled with the fruit – but no juice.

# Broiled Ham with Pineapple-Brown Sugar Sauce

**Sauce ingredients: (for up to 6 servings)**
  1 small can crushed pineapple
  ½ cup brown sugar
  ⅓ cup mustard

Combine all ingredients, including the pineapple juice. Figure one-half pound slices of ham per serving (but this is so good your guests or family may want more!) Use pre-cooked ham only, about ½ to ¾ inch thick. (I like it thick).

Place slices under the broiler in your stove or on the grill. Turn after about 5 minutes. Brush the top side with about half the sauce. Broil another 5 minutes. Brush on the remaining sauce as you serve the ham.


## Ham with Apple Sauce in a Skillet

**Ingredients to serve 4:**
   2 pounds of pre-cooked ham about ¾ inch thick cut into 4 servings
   1 large, hard apple, peeled, cored and diced
   2 T brown sugar
   1 cup apple juice or cider
   2 T prepared mustard
   2 T minced onion
   1 cup pineapple juice (if not handy, use more apple juice)
   2 T corn starch
   vegetable oil or butter

Heat the ham in the oil on both sides in a large, non-stick skilled until warm through and through (about 4 minutes per side). Remove the ham and place all other ingredients in the skillet (medium heat) and cook 3 or 4 minutes, stirring all the while, until the apple is tender and the sauce starts to thicken. Return the ham to the skillet and heat again on both sides. Serve the sauce over the ham.


## Fried Pork Chops with Apple Sauce

**Ingredients to serve 4:**
   4 large pork chops with bone in or 6 boneless
   2 - #2 cans apple sauce
   2 T brown sugar
   2 T cinnamon
   vegetable oil
   salt and pepper

Season the chops with salt and pepper. Fry in oil in a skillet until brown on both sides (about 4-5 minutes on each side). Meanwhile, combine the apple sauce, cinnamon and brown sugar. When the chops have been browned, cover with the apple sauce mixture, cover and cook over medium heat 3 or 4 minutes or until sauce is steaming. Serve chops with sauce on top.

## Pork with Apricot Stir-fry

**Ingredients to serve 6:**
    2 pounds of pork steak, cut into narrow strips (no more than ½ inch)
    1 – 16 oz. can apricots
    3 T soy sauce
    1 cup water
    2 T cornstarch
    1 cup cauliflower florets
    1 cup broccoli florets
    1 onion, cut and broken into rings
    2 ribs celery, chopped
    1 tomato, diced
    3 T vegetable oil

Cut the apricots into quarters and set aside. Save ½ cup of the juice. Combine the soy sauce, water, apricot juice and cornstarch in a bowl; stir until smooth.
Sauté the pork strips in the vegetable oil in a large skillet for 3 or 4 minutes or until all pink disappears.
Add the broccoli, cauliflower and onion and stir-fry a few more minutes until tender.
Add the sauce and bring to a boil, then reduce heat and cook another couple of minutes until it starts to thicken.
Add apricots and diced tomatoes and continue to cook and stir for another 2 or 3 minutes so that the fruit and tomatoes will be hot. Serve over rice or "riced" potatoes.

# Pork Stir-fry with Vegetables and Orange Sections

**Ingredients to serve 4:**
  4 oranges, broken into sections (cut each section into 2 or 3 pieces)
  juice from 2 of the oranges
  1 t zest from 1 of the oranges
  1 pound pork tenderloin, sliced fairly thin
  1 t salt
  ½ t pepper
  3 T olive oil (may substitute vegetable oil)
  4 cups vegetables of your choosing, broken or cut bite-size.
  (Asparagus, broccoli, celery, cauliflower or tiny, whole potatoes all
  work well)

Add the oil to a non-stick skillet along with the sliced pork and half
the salt and pepper and stir-fry until the pork loses all pink color.
Remove the pork with a slotted spoon and set aside.
Add the vegetables to the skillet, along with the balance of the seasonings and the orange juice and zest. Stir-fry until the vegetables are tender. Return meat to the skillet and stir-fry until meat is hot. Combine
all ingredients, including oranges and serve.
If you do not have a large enough skillet, the meal may be cooked in
batches.

# Pork Steak and Apples

**Ingredients to serve 4:**
  2 pounds of pork steak – ½ to ¾ inch thick
  5 apples, peeled, cored and sliced
  cinnamon
  salt and pepper
  vegetable oil
  water

Grease the bottom of a baking dish with vegetable or other oil to prevent sticking.

Scatter apple slices over the bottom of the baking dish. Sprinkle with cinnamon. Add a layer of pork steaks. Sprinkle with salt and pepper. Add more apple slices and sprinkle with cinnamon. Add the rest of the steak and sprinkle with salt and pepper. Add the rest of the apples slices and sprinkle with cinnamon.

Cover (barely) with water.

Bake in a 350 degree oven, uncovered, for 2 hours or until meat is tender.


## Pork Chops with Pears

**Ingredients to serve** 4:
   4 thick pork chops
   salt and pepper
   1 – 16 oz. can spiced pear halves (save liquid)

Salt and pepper the chops and cook them on the grill.

Meanwhile, dice the pears and cook them in the liquid from the can until "syrupy".

Serve the pear sauce over the chops.


## Pork Chops with Apricots

**Ingredients to serve** 4:
   4 large pork chops
   1 small jar apricot jam (marmalade)
   24 fresh or dried apricots, pitted and diced
   cooking oil
   salt and pepper

Cover the bottom of a large skillet with about ¼ inch of vegetable oil. Arrange the pork chops in the skillet. Lightly season the chops with salt and pepper. Lightly brown the chops and then turn them over. Spread apricot jam (if not available, peach will do) over the chops. Scatter the diced apricots over the chops. Cover and cook over medium heat until tender.

# Stuffed Pork Loin

**Ingredients to serve 6:**
   3# pork loin
   salt and pepper

**Stuffing ingredients:**
   1 cup chopped nuts (almonds, pecans or walnuts)
   2 T chopped onion

Cut the loin almost in two – lengthwise. With a meat mallet, pound the loin into a thickness of about ¾ inch. Season lightly with salt and pepper. Combine the stuffing ingredients thoroughly.
Spoon the stuffing over the meat, leaving about a 1 inch margin on the edges. Roll up the meat and tie with twine about every inch.
Roast in a pre-heated 400 degree oven for 45 minutes or until a meat thermometer inserted into the center registers 160 degrees.
Cut crossways into 6 servings.


# Pork Loin Roast Topped with Apples

**Ingredients to serve 8:**
   4 to 5 pound pork loin
   3 medium apples, peeled, cored and diced fine
   ⅔ cup brown sugar
   1 T ground cinnamon
   salt and pepper

Rub the roast with salt and pepper. Combine the apples, brown sugar and cinnamon and spoon over the top of the roast.
Bake 3 hours in a 350 degree oven, uncovered.


# Chicken with Crunchy Cashew Crust

**Ingredients to serve 4:**
   4 chicken breasts, skinned and removed from the bone
   2 cups finely chopped cashews
   salt and pepper

Lightly season breasts with salt and pepper. Literally press the cashew pieces into the meat.

Bake in an uncovered baking dish in a 350 degree, pre-heated oven for 1 hour, turning after 30 minutes.

## Grilled Chicken Breasts with Peach Basting Sauce

**Ingredients to serve 4:**
  4 chicken half-breasts without the bone, skinned
  2 ripe peaches, pitted, peeled and diced
  1-½ cups water
  3 T cornstarch
  3 T gelatin powder (peach flavored if available)
  1-¼ cups sugar

Combine water, sugar and cornstarch in a saucepan; stir until smooth, bring to a boil, reduce heat and cook 2 more minutes, stirring occasionally.

Remove from stove and stir in the gelatin and diced peaches. Divide the sauce into 2 equal portions. Use half to baste the chicken breasts as they are grilled; use the other half to pour over the chicken when served.

## Oven-Fried Chicken with Pecan Crust

**Ingredients for baking parts of a medium to large chicken:**
  Separate chicken into its several parts: thighs, drumsticks, breasts, etc.

**Prepare a coating from the following ingredients;**
  ⅔ cup pecans, chopped fine
  ½ cup all-purpose flour
  ⅔ cup cornmeal or crushed cracker crumbs or "shore lunch"
  1 t salt

Dice ½ stick butter (⅛ pound).

Prepare an egg wash by beating 2 eggs into a cup of water.

Combine the coating ingredients in a large bowl. Dip each chicken piece into the egg wash and then roll in the coating ingredients until well covered. Place in a lubricated baking pan or dish, dot with butter pieces and bake in a pre-heated 400 degree oven for an hour and fifteen minutes or until pieces are a golden brown.

# Chicken on the Grill with Pineapple Sauce

**Ingredients to serve 4:**
  1 chicken, cut into parts, leaving skin on
  1 can crushed pineapple
  ½ cup orange juice
  ½ cup honey
  1 t ground ginger

Combine last 4 ingredients into a basting sauce. Lightly baste all sides of the chicken parts and place on the grill skin side down. (Too much sauce will cause the flames to shoot up). Turn once, after about 8 minutes. Continue grilling until juices run clear. Baste with remaining sauce before serving. Thicker pieces take a little longer.

# Chicken with Pecans and Peppers

**Ingredients to serve 4:**
  2 chicken breasts (4 half-breasts) cubed bite-size
  ½ stick butter (⅛ pound)
  2 bell peppers, one green the other red, seeded and cut into narrow
    strips
  1-½ cups pecan halves
  2 T minced garlic
  ½ cup vinegar (preferably balsamic)
  2 T sugar
  salt to taste

Melt the butter. Sauté the pepper strips (briefly) until soft. Add the garlic and a dash of salt and continue cooking and stirring for another minute. Remove pepper strips to a bowl using a slotted spoon.
There should be some butter remaining in the skillet, if not, add a little (1 T). Add the vinegar and 2 Ts sugar to the skillet. Continue to cook and stir until reduced to about half. Sauté the cubed chicken in the vinegar-butter mixture until brown on all sides – check to be sure they are cooked through.
Serve chicken with peppers and nuts on top. Drizzle any remaining liquid in the pan over the chicken pieces.

# Glazed Chicken with Fruit and Rice

**Ingredients to serve 4:**
  2 chicken breasts (4 half-breasts) cubed bite-size
  4 T vegetable oil
  1 can chicken broth plus 1 can water
  3 T brown sugar
  3 T soy sauce
  2-½ cups white rice
  1 t cinnamon
  4 T chopped onions
  2 cups chopped fruit, such as: dried apricots, raisins, prunes, fresh pineapple, etc.

Sauté the cubed chicken (about 5 minutes) then reduce heat to medium and add brown sugar, onion and soy sauce and continue to cook about 2 minutes, stirring occasionally. Remove chicken with a slotted spoon.
Add chicken broth plus equal amount of water, also add rice and cinnamon. Cover, bring to a boil, then reduce heat to simmer and cook until rice is tender and liquid has been absorbed.
Remove from heat; add fruit, cover and let sit for 3 or 4 minutes before serving.

# Chicken Salad

This recipe could have been included in the salad chapter but it is really a main dish or meal in itself.

**Ingredients to serve 6:**
  1-½ to 2 pounds left-over (cooked) chicken, cubed
  1 cup seedless grapes, halved
  2 cans pineapple chunks, drained
  2 cans Mandarin orange sections, drained
  2 ribs celery, chopped
  1 sweet onion, chopped
  ½ cup black, pitted olives, sliced
  1 green pepper, seeded and chopped or cut into thin strips
  1 cup mayonnaise
  ½ cup sour cream
  1 t pepper
  1 t salt

Blend together the sour cream and mayonnaise (More may be needed, depending on how much chicken is used). Keep refrigerated.

Combine all other ingredients, taking care to distribute the salt and pepper evenly. Refrigerate at least one hour.

Blend the mayo-sour cream thoroughly with the other ingredients and serve chilled.

May be served as is or with chow mein noodles.


## Stuffed Baked Eggplant*

**Ingredients to serve 6 or 8:**
- 1-½ pounds lean ground beef
- 2 medium onions, finely chopped
- 2 medium eggplants
- 1 t salt (or to taste)
- 1 scant t cinnamon
- ½ t pepper (or to taste)
- 1 – 15 oz. can tomato paste, mixed with 1 can water
- ⅓ cup walnuts (chopped) or pine nuts
- vegetable oil

Skin eggplants.

Cut eggplants into at least one inch thick slices ending with about 4 slices per plant.

Brush with vegetable oil and place in pan under broiler or on outside grill until a light brown.

Sauté meat, onions and spices. Remove from skillet and sauté nuts until about half-done (not too brown).

Place meat mixture and nuts on top of eggplant slices in baking pan.

Pour tomato sauce over all.

Bake covered for about 1 hour at 375 degrees.

Serve with rice.

*Courtesy Don Droubie, Staples, MN

# Meat Pies (A Middle East Recipe)*

**Ingredients to serve 8 or 16 pies:**
  1 can Pillsbury Grand biscuit dough (or make your own dough)
  2-½ pounds lean ground beef
  2 finely chopped onions
  1 t salt
  1 t pepper
  10 T lemon juice
  1 cup pine nuts or chopped walnuts (contributor prefers pine nuts)

Mix all ingredients together and place about 1-½ T filling in the center of each 4 inch section of dough and pinch edges together to form a triangle, thus enclosing the filling completely. Place the triangle shaped meat pies side by side on a lightly oiled baking pan. Bake for 1 hour at 375 degrees or until bottoms of pies are brown. Then place under the broiler to brown the tops.

*Courtesy Don Droubie, Staples, MN

# Pineapple Meatball Sauce

Prepare meatballs from about 2 pounds hamburger using your favorite recipe. Bake the meatballs in the following sauce:

**Ingredients:**
  2 – 14 oz. cans crushed pineapple
  2 cups brown sugar
  3 T mustard
  2 T vinegar
  1 T soy sauce

Combine all ingredients in a baking dish. Place meatballs in the sauce. Bake in medium oven, covered, until well done. Test after 40 minutes.

# Orange Sauce with Ducks or Geese

**Ingredients:**
  1 cup orange juice
  ¼ cup lemon or lime juice
  2 T minced onion
  2 T chopped parsley or favorite herbs (thyme, tarragon, etc.)
  ¼ pound butter (1 stick)
  salt and pepper

Mix together all ingredients except the butter, salt and pepper. Pour over fillets and marinate 1 hour. Drain the fillets, season them with salt and pepper and sauté them in melted butter.
The marinade may be boiled down to about ½ the volume and served with the duck or goose.

# Raspberry Sauce

(Makes venison, duck, pork, veal or lamb taste special!)

**Ingredients for enough sauce for 4 servings of meat:**
  4 cups raspberries, fresh or frozen-thawed
  1 apple, cored, peeled and diced (fine)
  4 T sugar
  6 T grape juice (preferably white)
  4 servings of the meat of your choosing prepared as you wish

Use a blender to make the raspberries into a puree. Strain out the seeds. Transfer raspberry puree to a saucepan. Add diced apple, sugar and grape juice, stirring until smooth.
Bring to a boil, then reduce heat to simmer for five minutes or until apple is tender, stirring frequently. Serve hot over meat.

# Grape Hot Sauce

May be served over either big game cuts or with ducks.

**Ingredients for 2 ducks or 4 pounds of steaks or chops:**
    4 T butter, melted
    ½ cup chopped onion or green onions
    ½ cup grape jelly (other tart jellies may be substituted)
    1 cup red wine
    ¼ t Tabasco sauce

Sauté onion in 1 T butter. Stir in all other ingredients, adding the remainder of the butter last, one spoon at a time. Continue heating and stirring until the sauce thickens.

# Cider Sauce

Serve over chops or steaks.

**Ingredients for 1-½ pounds of steaks or chops:**
    1 T butter
    1 large, hard, red apple – peeled and chopped
    1 small chopped onion
    ½ cup cider
    salt and pepper to taste

Melt the butter and sauté the apple and onion a few minutes until tender. Add cider; continue to cook and stir until the sauce thickens. Serve over steaks or chops.

# Berry Sauce for Wild Game

Works well with venison, moose, ducks or geese.

**Ingredients:**
  4 cups blackberries (other berries may be substituted)
  2 hard apples, cored, peeled and diced fine
  2 cups brandy (wine may be substituted)
  ½ cup sugar
  ½ stick butter (⅛ pound)

Place the diced apples, brandy, sugar and butter in a saucepan. Bring to a boil and continue to cook until reduced to about 1 cup. Add the berries and stir gently until well coated.
Pour over each serving of meat while still hot.


# Orange and Honey Sauce

For Ducks, Geese or Big Game steaks or chops.

**Ingredients for 2 ducks or 8 big game chops:**
  3 T honey
  3 T orange juice concentrate
  2 T minced onion
  1 cup cream
  1 cup red wine (or red wine vinegar)
  salt and pepper to taste
  2 T butter, melted

Sauté onion in melted butter. Stir in all other ingredients and cook over medium heat until it comes to a boil. Lower heat and simmer 5 minutes, while stirring.
Brush ⅓ sauce on birds or chops while cooking and serve the balance with the meal.

# USING FRUIT AND OR NUTS IN DRESSING (STUFFING)

## Walnuts and Raspberries in Dressing

Ingredients to serve 4:
    2 cups seasoned croutons (or cubed day-old bread)
    4 T chopped onion
    4 T diced celery
    1 egg
    1 stick butter (¼ pound) melted
    ½ cup toasted walnuts, chopped
    1 cup raspberries
    2 T vinegar (raspberry flavored if available)

Combine croutons, onion, celery and walnuts in a bowl. Beat together the egg, melted butter and vinegar and stir into the crouton mixture until evenly distributed. Gently fold in the raspberries.
Bake in an oven-safe, covered dish in a 350 degree oven for 30 minutes. All or part of the dressing could be stuffed in a bird.

## Wild Rice-Apple-Cranberry-Pecan Dressing

Ingredients:
    1 cup wild rice
    4 cups water
    1 T salt
    3 cups seasoned croutons (or cubed day-old bread, toasted)
    ¼ pound butter (1 stick), melted
    2 apples, cored and diced
    4 ribs celery, chopped
    1 large onion, chopped
    1 cup chopped cranberries (dried or fresh)
    1 cup chopped pecans
    1 cup chicken broth
    2 cups chopped bologna or brats

**Seasonings:**
   2 t chopped sage
   2 t chopped marjoram
   1 t chopped thyme
   1 t freshly ground pepper
   2 t poultry seasoning

Place wild rice in the 4 cups of water, bring to a boil, then reduce heat to simmer and cover for 1-½ hours or until rice "flowers."
Drain rice in colander.
Combine all ingredients in oven-proof dish, cover and bake in pre-heated 375 degree oven for 20 minutes, then remove cover and continue to bake for another 20 minutes or until top is a golden brown.

## Nutty Wild Rice Stuffing

**Ingredients:**
   1 cup wild rice
   ½ cup chopped nuts (almonds, pecans, hazelnuts, walnuts or a combination)
   1 can water chestnuts, sliced
   ¼ pound fresh mushrooms (or a 4 oz. can)
   1 onion, chopped
   ½ cup celery, chopped
   ⅛ pound butter
   1 t sage
   salt and pepper to taste

Prepare the wild rice by any of the basic recipes*. Sauté the onion, celery and fresh mushrooms in butter over low heat. Mix together all ingredients, thoroughly, as you season to taste.
*or – add 4 cups of water to the rice, bring to a boil; reduce heat, cover, and let simmer 1-½ hours. (check occasionally for dryness).

# Orange Flavored Wild Rice Stuffing with Nuts

**Ingredients:**
¾ cup wild rice
⅛ pound butter
2 T orange peel, grated
½ cup celery, chopped
½ cup green pepper, chopped
¼ cup walnuts, chopped
juice of 1 orange
½ cup seasoned bread crumbs
1 T melted butter
salt and pepper to taste

Prepare the rice by any of the basic methods or by the method described in the previous recipe.
Sauté the celery and green pepper a few minutes in the butter.
Mix together all the ingredients, including the butter used to sauté the celery and green pepper. Season to taste.
Ladle the stuffing into the vegetable of your choice. Hollowed out oranges also work very well with this recipe. Stir the melted butter and seasoned bread crumbs together and sprinkle them on top. Bake in medium oven,
350 degrees until the vegetable is tender.

# MARINADES

Warning: If marinades are saved to serve with fish or game, boil first.

## South Seas Marinating Sauce*

Will marinate 2 pounds of steaks. Adds a unique and special flavor.

**Ingredients:**
- ½ cup salad oil
- 2 T soy sauce
- ½ cup orange juice
- ¼ cup sugar
- ¼ cup finely chopped onion
- ½ t salt
- ½ t pepper
- 4 T sesame seeds

Place steaks in single layer in a shallow dish or pan. Combine all ingredients and pour over steaks. Let stand, refrigerated, 6 hours, turn steaks and let marinate another 6 hours. If you suspect the steaks are tough, let marinate up to 24 hours.

*Courtesy Darlene Dokken, Colorado

# Citrus-Cider Marinade

Use for any variety of big game (roasts or steaks).

**Ingredients:**
- 3 lemons, juice of
- 1 large orange, juice of
- 2 cups cider
- ½ cup vinegar
- 1 medium onion, chopped
- ½ T nutmeg

Combine all ingredients. Turn meat several times during treatment. Let stand refrigerated 24 hours or up to 3 days for really tough meat.

# Orange-Cognac Marinade

For Ducks, Geese or Big Game.

**Ingredients for 2 mallards:**
  1 cup orange juice
  ½ cup cognac
  2 T Madeira
  1 small onion, chopped fine
  1 T grated orange peel
  1 t fresh thyme (or ½ t dried)
  1 t fresh rosemary (or ½ t dried)
  salt and pepper to taste

Combine all ingredients, adding salt and pepper to taste. Marinate ducks 24 hours, turning birds approximately every 8 hours with the breasts being the down side 16 hours.
Save the marinade and use to baste the birds in the oven; it also may be served with the birds.

# CHAPTER VII

# FRUIT AND/OR NUTS WITH FISH

# Fried Freshwater Fillets with Almonds

A gourmet sensation.

**Ingredients:**
 2 eggs
 1 T milk
 1-½ pounds perch or pike fillets, cut into serving pieces
 ½ t salt
 freshly ground black pepper
 ½ cup flour
 1 cup almonds, pulverized in a blender or with a nut grinder
 4 T butter
 2 T vegetable oil
 2 lemons, each cut lengthwise into quarters

In a small shallow bowl, beat the eggs lightly with a whisk or table fork and mix in the milk. Pat the fish completely dry with paper towels and sprinkle with the salt and a few grindings of pepper. Spread the flour on one piece of wax paper and the nuts on another. Dip the fillets in the flour, than shake gently to remove the excess. One at a time, immerse the filets in the egg mixture and then place them on the nuts, turning them over until they are evenly coated on both sides. Arrange the fillets in one layer on wire cake racks set over a cookie sheet. Refrigerate for at least 30 minutes. When you are ready to fry the fish, melt the butter with the oil in a heavy or Teflon skillet over moderate heat. When the foam begins to subside, add 3 or 4 fillets, depending on their size. Fry the fillets for 3 to 5 minutes on each side turning them with a spatula. When done they should be crisp and brown and feel firm to the touch. Transfer to a heated platter and garnish with the quartered lemons.

# Baked Freshwater Fillets with Pecan Crust

**Ingredients to serve 4:**
 2 pounds perch fillets, skinned
 1 cup breadcrumbs
 1 cup pecans, chopped
 ¼ pound butter, melted
 salt and lemon pepper to taste
 cooking oil, butter or margarine

Arrange the fillets on a well oiled baking sheet. Season with salt and lemon pepper. Sprinkle generously with breadcrumbs and chopped pecans. Drizzle the melted butter over the crumbs.

Bake in a pre-heated 300 degree oven for about 20 minutes or until the crumbs are a crusty brown.

## Trout Amandine

A restaurant favorite; here's how they do it:

**Ingredients:**
  4 trout fillets
  flour and salt
  ½ cup butter
  ½ t onion juice
  ¼ cup blanched, finely slivered almonds
  1 T lemon juice

Wash and dry the fish. Dust with salt and flour. Heat half the butter and onion juice in a heavy skilled and cook fish until lightly browned. Remove and place on a hot serving dish. Pour off the grease remaining in the pan and add the rest of the butter. Add the almonds and brown slowly, then add lemon juice and when it foams, pour it over the fish.

## Salmon with Lemon Slices and Dill Sauce

**Ingredients to serve 4:**
  1 – 2 pound salmon fillet with skin on
  1 lemon, sliced
  1 medium, sweet onion, peeled and sliced
  lemon pepper
  garlic salt (optional)
  1 stick butter (¼ pound)

**Ingredients for dill sauce:**
½ cup mayonnaise
½ cup sour cream
1 T dill weed
1 T lemon juice
1 T creamed horseradish

Place fillet on foil, skin side down. Lightly season with lemon pepper and garlic salt. Place about a half-dozen lemon slices and a like number of onion slices on the fillet. Dot with chunks of butter. Cook on the grill (uncovered) or in a pre-heated 350 degree oven. If you use the oven, bake it for about 20 minutes or until the salmon flakes easily. You want it done but not over-done.
Meanwhile prepare the dill sauce by combining all ingredients until smooth.

# Baked Northern with Raisin Stuffing

This recipe works equally well with muskies or whitefish. On the other hand, all fish are not good baked; even the tasty walleye or the flavorful bass are only fair unless they receive special treatment and seasonings. Northerns should weigh 5 pounds or more, whitefish at least 3.

**Preparing the fish:**
Scale and gut the fish; remove the head, tail and all fins. Wash and dry the fish, inside and out.
Score the back of the fish with cross section cuts about 3 inches apart, down to the backbone.
Salt and pepper, inside and out and in the cuts.

**Preparing the stuffing:**
1 cup raisins
¼ pound butter (added to 1 cup hot water)
2 cups croutons or dry bread crumbs
1 large onion, chopped but not too fine
salt and pepper
1 cup chopped bologna (or wieners or polish sausage or luncheon meat)

Place the croutons, raisins, meat and onions in a bowl. Salt and pepper lightly while stirring the ingredients together.

Add and stir in the butter-hot water mixture just before stuffing the fish. Lay a sheet of foil on the bottom of the roaster.

Stuff the fish (loosely) and place upright on the sheet of foil. Fold the foil up along both sides of the fish, do not cover the back. The foil will hold in the stuffing. If your fish is too long for the roaster, you may cut it in two and bake the two sections side by side.

Leftover stuffing or additional stuffing may be baked in a foil package alongside the fish or even outside the roaster.

Place a strip of bacon and a slice of onion, alternately, over each score (or cut).

Cover the roaster and place in a pre-heated 300 degree oven. After 1 hour, remove cover and continue to bake until the meat becomes flaky and separates from the backbone (as viewed from the end of the fish). This should take about another ½ hour, depending on the size of the fish.

Transfer the baked fish to a platter. Cut through the backbone at each score mark, separating the fish into serving size portions. The stuffing may be lifted out with each portion as it is served.

Serve with tartar sauce and/or lemon.

## Lemon Rubbed and Wine Basted Baked Fish with Wild Rice Dressing

Choose a large northern pike or whitefish. Scale and draw the fish; remove the heat, tail and fins; wash thoroughly inside and out and dry. Strain the juice of 3 lemons; salt lightly. Rub the inside and the outside of the fish, thoroughly, with the salted lemon juice.

Refrigerate the fish for 2 or 3 hours.

**Prepare stuffing:**
   1 cup wild rice, washed (will make 3 cups cooked rice)*
   ½ cup melted butter or margarine mixed with ½ cup hot water
   l large onion, chopped
   ⅓ pound chopped bologna or summer sausage or polish sausage or luncheon meat
   1 cup celery, chopped
   1 small green pepper (or 1/3 cup)

## Cook the wild rice:
    3 cups of water
    1 cup wild rice (washed)
    salt and pepper
    ¼ pound melted butter or margarine

Season water with 1 T salt and bring to a boil. Add rice and lower the heat so that the water just simmers. Cook, covered, for about 1-½ hours or until the kernels are well opened and the rice is tender. Do not overcook.

Pour off any water that has not been absorbed. Add pepper and a little more salt to taste; pour on the melted butter and fluff with a fork.

## Sauté the celery and onions:
Cook slowly in butter or margarine for about 3 minutes or until the onions are translucent and the celery is light brown.

## Combine:
The wild rice, onion, celery, chopped meat and green pepper. Season lightly with salt and pepper. Pour ½ cup melted butter combined with an equal amount of hot water over the mixture and stir the ingredients together, thoroughly.

## Stuff and bake:
Pat the chilled fish dry and stuff loosely. Left over dressing may be baked separately in foil along side the fish. Place a sheet of foil in the bottom of a roaster, then place the fish in the roaster (back up). Bring the foil up half way around the fish to hold in the stuffing. Place in a pre-heated medium oven, 350 degrees.

Melt ¼ pound of butter and add an equal amount of white wine. Baste fish from time to time with the wine-butter mixture.

Bake until the meat flakes easily from the large end of the fish (about 15 minutes per pound).

Transfer baked fish to serving platter; garnish with parsley and serve with lemon wedges.

# Stuffed Fish with a Touch of Lemon

4 fish fillets (1-½ pounds each)

**Ingredients:**
 ½ cup finely chopped celery
 ¼ cup chopped onion
 3 T butter
 4 cups dry bread cubes or croutons
 ½ t grated lemon peel
 4 t lemon juice
 1 T snipped parsley
 1 T butter, melted

Place 2 fillets in a greased baking pan. Cook celery and onion in 3 T butter until crisp tender. Pour over bread. Add lemon peel and juice, parsley, ½ t salt and a dash of pepper and toss together. Spoon half the stuffing mixture on each fillet in the pan.
Top with remaining 2 pieces of fish, brush with 1 T butter. Sprinkle with salt and paprika and bake, covered at 350 degrees for about 25 minutes.

# Banana-Chutney Sauce with Fish (A Caribbean recipe)

Especially good over white meated fish.

**Ingredients for about 2 pounds fillets:**
 1 banana, sliced thin
 ½ cup chutney, chopped fine
 1 T butter
 ½ cup banana liqueur
 ¼ cup water
 salt and pepper to taste

Place all the ingredients in a saucepan and bring to a boil. Remove from heat and add seasonings to taste.

# Salt Water Fillets with Almond and Marmalade Coating

Works well with grouper, salmon, red snapper, etc. May be a little too strong a flavor for freshwater fish, except bass.

**Ingredients to serve 4:**
   2 pounds of fillets, skinned and deboned
   1 cup orange marmalade
   ½ cup slivered almonds
   ⅓ cup chopped green onions (both white and green parts)
   ¼ t garlic salt
   ½ t black pepper

Place the fillets in a lubricated baking dish or pan.
Combine the marmalade, onions, salt and pepper; mix thoroughly.
Spread mixture evenly over the fillets.
Bake in a pre-heated 400 degree oven, uncovered, for 15 minutes or until the fish flakes easily.
Sprinkle with almonds before serving.

*You may substitute 1 cup raisins for the wild rice and add 1-½ cups croutons. You could also use ½ white and ½ wild rice.

# CHAPTER VIII

# FRUIT SALSAS WITH FISH OR GAME

# FRUIT SALSAS

Fruit Salsas are served as an accompaniment to meats such as pork, fish or poultry, but they may also be used as a dip.

## Pineapple-Orange-Cranberry Salsa

Ingredients:
    1 large (#2) can crushed pineapple
    1 cup orange juice
    1 can (#2) cranberry sauce
    2 t lemon juice
    ½ t garlic salt
    1 t ground ginger
    1 t ground allspice

Thoroughly combine all ingredients.

## Peach (or Apricot) Salsa #1

Ingredients:
    2 cups chopped peaches or apricots
    1 cup minced cucumber (first peel and seed)
    2 cups chili sauce

Thoroughly combine all ingredients.

## Peach Salsa #2

Ingredients:
    3 peaches, peeled, pitted and chopped
    1 small can (5-½ oz.) pineapple tidbits
    ¾ cup green chilies, chopped fine (use kitchen gloves for hot varieties)
    1 medium onion, chopped
    1 avocado, peeled, pitted and chopped
    1 T chopped (fine) garlic
    1 T lemon juice

Combine all ingredients and refrigerate.

# Chutney Fruit Salsa

**Ingredients:**
    1 cup chutney of your choice
    1 cup chopped honeydew melon meat
    4 medium tomatoes, skinned and chopped
    4 Jalapeno peppers, chopped (use rubber gloves)
    1 medium onion, chopped
    2 T chopped cilantro
    ¼ t salt
    ½ T pepper

Chop and thoroughly mix all ingredients.


# Banana Salsa

**Ingredients for 1-½ cups:**
    1 large, ripe (but not over-ripe) banana, cut into small pieces
    1 small green or red bell pepper, seeded and diced
    2 T minced fresh mint
    1 green onion (use white portion only) chopped
    2 T lime juice (or lemon)
    1-½ T brown sugar

Combine all ingredients thoroughly.


# Date-Raisin Salsa

**Ingredients:**
    1 cup chopped (pitted first) dates
    1 cup raisins
    2 cups chili sauce
    4 T orange juice
    ½ t Tabasco sauce

Combine all ingredients thoroughly.

## Cherry Salsa

**Ingredients:**
  1 cup cherry jam
  4 T minced onion
  4 T minced green pepper
  4 T chopped green chilies
  1 t minced garlic

Combine all ingredients thoroughly. Cover and chill 24 hours.

## Pineapple-Peach Salsa

**Ingredients:**
  1 small can crushed pineapple, including the juice
  2 peaches, pitted, peeled and chopped
  1 t minced garlic
  1 green chili pepper, chopped
  ½ t ground ginger

Combine all ingredients thoroughly. Refrigerate, covered, at least 4 hours.

## Apricot Salsa

**Ingredients:**
  1 cup chopped apricots (pitted and peeled)
  ½ cup chopped avocado
  ½ t minced garlic
  1-½ T chopped cilantro
  ½ t red pepper flakes
  4 T lemon juice

Combine all ingredients thoroughly. Cover and refrigerate 24 hours.

# Fruity Hot Sauce

**Ingredients:**
  2 avocados, peeled and mashed
  10 small, hot peppers, chopped (use rubber gloves)
  ½ cup brown sugar
  1 T chili powder
  4 T Dijon mustard
  1 t curry powder
  4 T onion, minced
  2 T garlic, minced

In a blender, puree the avocados. Change speed to "slow" and blend in all other ingredients.

# CHAPTER IX

# WILD FRUITS AND BERRIES

# WILD FRUITS AND BERRIES

Wild fruits and berries are usually more flavorful than their cultivated counterparts; however, they tend to be more tart and therefore will require more sugar than traditional recipes. Otherwise, your favorite treatments for sauces, pies, jellies and jams will work very well. Most of the recipes found in this chapter are appropriate for nearly all of the wilderness fruits and berries, including chokecherries, blueberries, raspberries, strawberries, blackberries and June berries.

## Chokecherry Syrup

Great on pancakes, waffles or French toast or as a topping for ice cream.

**Ingredients:**
  4 cups berries
  2 cups water
  2 cups sugar

Place berries and water together in a kettle; bring to a boil, reduce heat so that the liquid will boil slowly until the chokecherries are soft. Force the mixture through a sieve. Stir in sugar and return to stove; let simmer, stirring constantly until it thickens. Remember the thickening will increase as the mixture cools. Pour into sterilized glass jars and seal. If the syrup will be kept under refrigeration or in a cool place, an ordinary screw cap such as found on mayonnaise jars will suffice. This recipe also works well with most other berries but in the case of blueberries or strawberries, for example, you may prefer not to strain out the pulp.

## Chokecherry and Wine Jelly

**Ingredients:**
  1 cup Chokecherry juice (or use 2 cups of chokecherry syrup and
    omit the sugar)
  1 cup red wine
  3 cups sugar
  ½ bottle liquid pectin

To make the juice, cover the berries with water, bring to a boil and then let simmer until the berries soften. Force through a sieve or jelly bag. Mix the juice, wine and sugar in a kettle until the sugar dissolves. Bring to a boil as you stir; let boil 1 minute (continue stirring). Remove from the stove and gradually stir in the pectin. Ladle into pre-heated jars or jelly glasses.
Seal (paraffin will do).

## Blueberry Jelly*

Ingredients:
  2 cups blueberry juice (make juice by following procedure explained for chokecherries)
  4 cups sugar
  1 t lemon juice (or whatever citrus juice you have handy)
  1 bottle fruit pectin

Stir the juice, sugar and lemon juice together until the sugar dissolves. Bring to a boil. Add a restaurant size pat of butter to reduce foaming. Stir constantly. After the mixture comes to a full boil, remove from heat and add pectin. Return to the stove and let boil 1 minute, stirring all the while. Skim off any foam. Ladle into heated sterilized jelly glasses and seal with paraffin.

## Blueberry Jam

Ingredients:
  4 cups cleaned blueberries
  5 cups sugar
  1 cup water

Mix together the above ingredients. Bring to a boil and then reduce heat so that it will boil slowly, for 15 minutes or until thick. Stir all the while, crushing the berries occasionally with a spoon. If the mixture is too dry at any point to boil freely, add a little water. Ladle into sterilized glasses or jars and seal.

# Blueberry Sauce

Most any wild berries may be used with this updated version of an old favorite recipe.

**Ingredients:**
   4 cups berries (carefully picked over and cleaned)
   ⅔ cup sugar
   3 T cornstarch (flour may be substituted)
   2 cups water (hot)
   2 T lemon or other citrus juice
   ½ t salt
   2 pats butter

Combine the sugar, cornstarch and salt.
Add the lemon juice to the hot water. Stir this mixture, a little at a time, into the dry mixture. When it is smooth, place over low heat and cook until it thickens, stirring occasionally.
Add blueberries and continue simmering until the sauce has the desired "thickness", remembering that it will thicken still more as it cools.
Remove from the stove and stir in the butter as it melts.
This also makes an excellent syrup; just continue the heating and stirring process until it is "syrupy".

*A blueberry pie recipe may be found on page 170

# Blueberry Muffins*

**Ingredients for 20-22 muffins:**
Cream together ½ cup butter (or margarine), 1-⅛ cup sugar and 2 eggs. Add 1 cup sour cream (can use no fat) or plain yogurt, 1 t vanilla, 2 cups of flour, 1 t baking powder, ½ t baking soda and ¼ t salt. Stir in a cup fresh blueberries. Bake 20 minutes at 400 degrees in muffin tins. Sprinkle with powdered sugar.

*Courtesy Carolyn Ring, Turtle Lake, Bemidji, MN

# Wild Cranberries

Minnesota has hundreds of wild cranberry bogs hidden away in tamarack and spruce swamps. Finding them is a real challenge and don't count on anyone showing you their favorite spot! The cranberries are often hidden under the foliage and defy detection. Oh yes, you'll need a pair of hip boots!

Once you find the cranberries, you may cook them with the very same recipes you use for those purchased in the supermarket. Here are a few that may be new to you, however:

## Cranberry Relish

Wash the berries and let dry.
Put them through a grinder or chopper, making a cranberry pulp.
For each cup of pulp add 1 cup of sugar. Stir until the sugar is completely blended into the pulp.
For a more tart flavor, add 2 T lemon or orange juice for each cup of pulp.
Serve with any wild game, but what could be better than wild cranberries with wild turkey or duck?

## Cranberry Stuffing

Use your favorite stuffing recipe but add 1 cup chopped raw cranberries.

## Pincherry Jelly

Extract the juice by adding 3 cups of water to 2 cups of berries. Simmer about 5 minutes as you mash the berries. Strain through a jelly bag or sieve.
Return the juice to the stove and bring to a boil. Then lower the temperature and let simmer 15 minutes, stirring regularly.
Remove from heat and add 1 bottle fruit pectin. Skim off foam and ladle into hot jelly glasses. Seal with paraffin.
The jelly will be clear and a very bright red.
A cup of red wine added during the last 15 minutes of simmering will give the jelly an exciting taste.

## Spicy Jams and Jellies

**Add ½ t each of:**
  ground cloves
  ground allspice
  ground cinnamon

Before the final boiling or simmering process starts. The spicy taste goes especially well with blueberry and rose hip jellies.

## Mixed Fruit Jellies

The juices of some berries and fruits may be combined to attain special textures and flavors. For example, apple juice may be added to chokecherries, wild plums, rose hips or wild grapes. Don't be afraid to experiment.

A combination that will have your family and guests guessing is to use equal parts of most any berry juice and sumac juice. To extract sumac juice, cover the red berries with water and boil a few minutes and then strain.

Sumac has been called the "lemonade of the wilderness".

## Plum Butter

Wash and remove blemished or spoiled areas.

Make plum pulp by covering the fruit with water (just barely) and then boil until the plums are soft. Force through a sieve or food mill.

To each cup of pulp, add ⅔ cup of sugar. Cook until thick, stirring regularly. It should take about a half-hour.

Ladle into pre-heated glasses and seal.

For a little spicier flavor, add a T of cinnamon and a T of cloves to each cup of pulp before cooking.

## Syrupy Wild Strawberry Sauce

This is especially good on shortcake, pancakes, waffles or ice cream. Wild strawberries are very small, but extremely flavorful and well worth the effort to pick.

**Ingredients:**
- 2 cups cleaned berries
- 1 t vinegar
- enough water to cover berries
- 1-½ cups sugar

Cover the strawberries with water, add the vinegar and boil for 1 minute. Stir in the sugar (thoroughly) and simmer 15 minutes. User fresh or preserve in sealed jars. It will keep several days under refrigeration, however.

Regular sauce may be made by using the same procedure, but do not simmer more than a few minutes.

## Wild Blackberry (Sometimes called Dewberry) Jam

**Ingredients:**
- 4 cups blackberries
- 6 cups sugar
- 1 orange, ground or chopped
- 1 lemon, ground or chopped
- 1 cup water
- a dash of baking soda (fraction teaspoon)
- 1 bottle fruit pectin

Combine the chopped lemon and orange with the soda and water. Simmer for 20 minutes. Do not let it dry out; in that case add a little more water.

Add berries and sugar. Stir together. Add enough water so that the mixture can boil freely. Bring to a boil and then reduce heat and let simmer 10 minutes.

Remove from heat and stir in the pectin.

Skim off foam and ladle into hot jars or jelly glasses.

# Wild Rice and Wild Berries

**Ingredients:**
½ cup wild rice
2-½ cups water
1 small can crushed pineapple
1 cup raspberries or strawberries (wild, if you can find them)
1 cup blueberries
4 T sugar
whipped cream for topping

Prepare wild rice by adding 2-½ cups of water, bring to a boil, reduce heat to simmer, cover and cook for about 1-½ hours. Drain. Chill. Combine all ingredients and serve with whipped cream topping.

# CHAPTER X

# JUST NUTS

# KEEPING AND ENHANCING NUTTY FLAVOR

## Keeping Nuts:

Shelled nuts may be kept in air-tight containers (like ziplock bags) under refrigeration or frozen for months.

## Enhancing Flavor:

Warm nuts are more flavorful. Try toasting them on a baking sheet in a pre-heated 350 degree oven for about 10 minutes. A skillet with a little oil may be used but stir nuts frequently. They burn easily. See other recipes in this chapter for seasoning the nuts.

## Cayenne Flavored Nuts

Ingredients:
   4 cups of mixed nuts – such as cashews, almonds, pine nuts, shelled
      pistachios, pecans, etc.
   6 T vegetable oil (about ⅓ inch in bottom of skillet)
   3 T cumin seeds
   4 T sesame seeds
   1 T salt
   ½ t cayenne pepper
   ½ t finely ground black pepper

Pre-heat oil in skillet so that dropping a "test" nut in the pan sizzles. Add all ingredients except the seeds and cook for 2 minutes, stirring continuously. Add the seeds and continue cooking and stirring for about 30 seconds. Let drain and cool on paper towels.

# Spiced Nuts #1

**Try all or some of the following ingredients:**
  salt
  pepper
  cayenne pepper
  ground coriander
  dry mustard
  garlic salt
  sesame seeds

Use enough vegetable or olive oil to coat the nuts.
Pre-heat the oven to 325 degrees.
In a mixing bowl, coat the nuts of your choosing with the oil.
Sprinkle the seasonings of your choosing, one at a time, over the nuts, stirring while you sprinkle.
Spread the nuts on a baking sheet, single layer.
Roast in the oven 5 or 6 minutes. Remove from oven and let cool before serving.

# Spiced Nuts #2 (really hot!)

**Ingredients:**
  2 cups nuts of your choosing (walnuts, pecans and almonds all work well)
  4 T vegetable oil
  4 T Worcestershire sauce
  1 T chili powder
  1 t Tabasco or other hot sauce

Combine the nuts and vegetable oil in a bowl, stirring until the nuts are coated and there is no residue of oil in the bottom of the bowl. Scatter the nuts on a cookie sheet covered with foil. Bake in a pre-heated 350 degree oven for ten minutes.
Combine the Worcestershire sauce, chili powder and Tabasco in a bowl and sprinkle over the nuts. Return to the oven for another 10 minutes. Let cool some before serving so they aren't too hot to handle.

# Spiced Nuts #3

**Ingredients for 2 cups of mixed nuts of your choosing:**
  ½ cup sugar
  ¼ t ground allspice
  1 t ground cinnamon
  ½ t ground nutmeg
  3 T vegetable oil
  If nuts are not salted, add 1 t salt

Place the nuts in a bowl, sprinkle with vegetable oil and stir so nuts are well coated.
Combine dry ingredients, thoroughly, and sprinkle over nuts, stirring until nuts are all coated with spices.
Place nuts in a single layer on a baking sheet. Place in a pre-heated 350 degree oven for 5 minutes or under the broiler for 2 minutes. Cool before serving.

# Nut Popsicles

**Ingredients for 4 popsicles:**
  2 bananas
  1-½ cups nuts of your choosing
  ½ cup raisins
  1-½ cups water of your choosing
  1 cup honey

Combine all dry ingredients and 1 cup of water and blend at medium speed for 6 minutes.
Add the rest of the water, honey and bananas and blend another 4 minutes.
Pour into Popsicle molds and freeze.

# Nutty Dip for Veggies

**Ingredients to serve 4:**
  1 cup mixed nuts of your choosing
  ½ t chili powder
  3 t Worcestershire sauce
  1 T sesame seeds
  ½ t garlic powder
  ⅓ cup water
  dash of salt
  dash black pepper

Grind the nuts until almost powdery, (a coffee mill works well).
Combine all other ingredients, and then blend in the nuts.
Great for dipping broccoli, cauliflower, etc.


# Honey-Almond Spread

**Ingredients:**
  1 cup ground almonds (use a coffee mill)
  1 cup honey
  ½ cup water

Combine all ingredients; stir until thoroughly blended. Use as a spread on toast or other breads.


# Syrupy Nuts on Shortbread Cookies

**Ingredients to serve 6:**
  1 pkg. "store bought" shortbread cookies
  1 can deluxe mixed nuts
  1 cup white corn syrup or honey
  ½ cup brown sugar
  1 t vanilla extract
  1 stick butter (¼ pound), melted

Combine the syrup, brown sugar, vanilla extract and butter in a saucepan over low heat, stirring until the brown sugar dissolves. Stack 4 shortbread cookies per serving with mixed nuts in between cookies and on top. Spoon liquid over each stack.

# Sugared Nuts

**Ingredients for 4 cups of nuts:**
  4 cups of nuts of your choice; you may mix varieties
  1 cup sugar
  1 t salt
  2 t cinnamon
  2 T water
  1 egg – white part only

Combine egg white and water and beat until it is "frothy".
In a zip-lock plastic bag, combine sugar, salt and cinnamon, just shake.
Dip nuts in the egg white froth and then drop them into the plastic
bag and shake.
Place them on a well-lubricated baking sheet and bake in a pre-heated
350 degree oven for 30 minutes or until the coating is dry. Cool before
serving.

# Wild Nuts

Filberts, hazelnuts and butternuts all grow wild. They are ready for
picking in August or early fall when the shells are well formed, hard
and can be removed from the protecting foliage. The nuts may be
removed far easier, however, if the husks are dried first by placing them
on a garage or shed roof, in a single layer, where the sun can dry them
until the nuts almost fall out. Nuts may also be dried by packing them,
loosely, in the inside part of a minnow bucket and then hanging the
bucket from a tree limb. Nuts are best stored in their shells, but exam-
ine each for worm holes and discard those so infected or the worms
will move from nut to nut! A covered, gallon plastic or glass jar makes
an excellent container for storage.
Wild, cracked nuts make a great fireside snack on a winter night or
may be used in homemade cookies, candy, breads and cakes or may be
crushed for use as a dessert topping.
Acorns may also be eaten, but they are not as tasty, frankly, as the nuts
just described! But if you are interested in something a little different,
shell the acorns, let them soak in water overnight; and then roast them
in a slow oven with a mixture of milk and sugar. They may also be
chopped for use in baking.
Certain Indian tribes made a flour from the acorns and used them in
making a type of bread.

# CHAPTER XI

# FRUIT AND NUTS USED IN BAKING

# Blueberry and Wild Rice Muffins

**Ingredients for 12 muffins:**
¼ cup wild rice
2 cups water
½ cup blueberries
1-½ cups all purpose flour
1 cup milk
2 T sugar
1 egg
1 t baking powder
3 T soft shortening
2 T honey
2 t salt

Prepare the wild rice by adding the water and bringing it to a boil.
Reduce heat, cover and cook for 1-½ hours or until well "flowered".
Sift the dry ingredients.
Beat together the egg, milk and shortening.
Mix together all of the ingredients and spoon into greased muffin tins.
Bake in hot oven, 400 degrees, 15-20 minutes or until muffins are
golden.

# Wild Rice and Red River Cereal Bread

**Ingredients:**
¾ cup wild rice flour (may be made in blender; use puree position)
5 cups flour
2 cups Red River cereal (available mostly in Canada)
2 pkgs. dry yeast
3 T softened shortening
⅓ cup molasses
2 t salt
¼ cup brown sugar

Prepare cereal according to directions on the package.
Dissolve yeast.
Place cereal, wild rice flour, 2 cups white four, salt, brown sugar, shortening and molasses in large bowl; mix well.
Let sit a few minutes, and then knead in remainder of the white flour a cup at a time, until smooth. Place in greased bowl and cover.
Let rise in warm place until about double in volume. Knead air out.
Divide into loaves. Place in greased bread pans.
Bake in hot oven, 400 degrees, for 30 minutes or until done.

# Cranberry-Apple Crispies

**Ingredients:**
   4 cups frozen cranberries, chopped (may use fresh)
   4 cups apples, cored and sliced (quite thin)
   1 T cinnamon
   1 T all purpose flour
   ⅔ cup sugar
   1 T orange juice or zest, grated

**Ingredients for topping:**
   ¼ pound butter (1 stick) melted
   4 T brown sugar
   4 T flour, all purpose
   1 cup oatmeal, regular or quick, uncooked

Combine all ingredients in the top group and ladle into a 10 inch baking dish or pan, sprayed with cooking oil.
Combine topping ingredients and spread evenly over fruit mixture.
Bake in a pre-heated 375 degree oven for 35-40 minutes or until a light, golden brown. Check apple slices for tenderness.

# Blueberry Cobbler

**Ingredients to serve 4:**
　4 cups blueberries
　¼ cup water
　1 T orange zest (grated rind)
　1 T vanilla extract
　4 T sugar
　3 T cornstarch
　3 T water

**Ingredients for topping:**
　1 pie pastry shell, rolled out and divided into 4 pieces.
　3 T butter, melted

Combine blueberries, ¼ cup water, orange peel, vanilla and sugar in a saucepan. Heat and stir until bubbly and berries are cooked.
Combine the cornstarch and 3 T water and stir until smooth. Add to the ingredients in the saucepan.
Pour ingredients into 4, individual size oven proof dishes. Top with pastry, brushed with melted butter. Bake in a pre-heated 375 degree oven for 30 minutes or until a golden brown.

# Baklava-Quick and Easy

**Ingredients:**
　2 cans crescent dinner rolls (8 oz.)
　4 cups chopped pecans
　½ cup sugar
　2 T cinnamon

**Ingredients for a glaze:**
　½ cup honey
　½ cup sugar
　2 T lemon juice
　2 T butter, melted

Open one can of dough and unroll contents, arranging them in a rectangle in the bottom of a 9x10 inch baking dish or pan. It should run up the sides of the pan a half-inch or so. Close the perforations in the dough with your finger. Bake in a pre-heated oven for 5 minutes. Meanwhile, combine the pecans, sugar and cinnamon. Spoon the mixture over the baked crust.

Open the second can of dough and cover the pecan mixture, pressing the dough against the sides of the pan. Combine the glaze ingredients in a saucepan and bring to a boil. Spread about half the glaze over the top crust. Return to the oven and bake 30 minutes. Remove from oven and spoon the remaining glaze over the top.

Let cool, then cut into squares or diamonds and serve.

## Czechoslovakian Kolaches

**Ingredients for 4 dozen:**
   6 cups flour, all-purpose
   1-½ cups milk, lukewarm
   2 eggs
   ½ cup vegetable oil
   2 envelopes dry yeast, dissolved
   1 t salt
   vegetable oil to brush pastry

Try your favorite canned fillings. Possibilities include prunes, apricot, poppy seed, apple sauce or jams of various kinds. Cottage cheese is another option.

Starting with half the flour, add the eggs, milk, salt and oil. Mix well until dough is smooth. Add dissolved yeast and as much of the remaining flour as it takes to make the dough easy to handle (not sticky). Place dough on a floured surface and knead until smooth (8 to 10 minutes). Put in a large greased bowl. Bring greased side up. Cover with dish towel. Place somewhere warm (over 80 degrees) and let rise until size doubles. Punch down dough and divide into two portions. Cover one half and set aside. Cut off small chunks of dough about the size of a large walnut. Make them ball-shaped. Place the balls on a greased cookie sheet (about 12 to a sheet). Using your fingers, flatten the center of each ball, leaving a half-inch rim around the edges of the circle. Fill the center with filling (about 1T). Form and fill 2 kolaches, then form and fill 2 more, then 2 more, etc.

Bake at 400 degrees for about 10 minutes or until a light brown. Let cool on wire racks. Repeat the process with the second half of the dough.

# Hawaiian Banana Bread (in a bread machine)

**Ingredients:**
2 ripe bananas, mashed
3 T butter, melted
⅔ cup water (warm, but not boiling)
1 egg
3 full cups all purpose flour
4 T sugar
½ t salt
3 t dry yeast
1 cup Macadamia nuts, chopped

Place the ingredients in the bread machine as suggested in the book of instructions that came with the machine. Bake as instructed.


# Prune Tarts

**Ingredients:**
3 cups flour
1-½ cups whipping cream
½ t salt
1 T baking powder
½ pound butter, softened
1 pound prunes
½ cup sugar
1 T lemon juice

Whip the cream. Prepare the dough by mixing together the flour, salt and baking powder and sifting it into the cream. Stir thoroughly and then blend in the softened butter. Refrigerate dough 2 hours.
Cover prunes with water and cook until soft. Drain, remove pits and place in a blender until a puree consistency. Mix sugar and lemon juice into the prunes.
Roll the dough into a sheet about ⅓ inch thick. Cut into 3 inch squares. Cut the corner of each square halfway to the center. Place a tablespoon of prune puree in the center of each square. Bring half of each split corner over the prune filling towards the center of the square. Place tarts on an ungreased cookie sheet. Let stand while you pre-heat the oven to 400 degrees. Bake until brown, about 12 minutes.

# Crescent Rolls with Fruit and/or Nuts

Next time you make – or buy – crescent rolls, try rolling up a teaspoon of chopped nuts and/or chopped fruit (dried or fresh) in each roll before baking.

# Brown Betty

**Ingredients:**
   3 cups chopped apples (peeled and cored)
   ½ cup brown sugar, (compacted)
   2 cups bread crumbs
   3 T butter, melted
   4 T water
   1 t cinnamon

Stir the bread crumbs into the melted butter. Combine all ingredients and bake in a square or rectangular pan in a pre-heated 350 degree oven for 25 minutes.

# Fruitcake

**Ingredients:**
   1-½ cups dates, chopped
   1-½ cups raisins
   6 T butter
   3 cups flour
   2 cups boiling water
   1 T cinnamon
   ½ t cloves (ground)
   1-½ cups chopped nuts (of your choosing)
   1 small jar maraschino cherries
   1 t salt
   2 cups sugar

Combine the raisins, dates, sugar, butter and water. Simmer for 20 minutes, stirring occasionally. Let cool. Add remaining ingredients. Bake in a loaf pan in a pre-heated 325 degree oven for 1-½ hours. May be stored, wrapped in foil and refrigerated or frozen.

# Fruit Cake – With a Touch of Coffee

**Ingredients:**
 2 cups cold coffee (need not be fresh brewed)
 1 pound raisins
 1 pound candied fruit
 2 cups chopped nuts of your choosing
 1 jar (about 8 oz.) maraschino cherries (including juice)
 3 cups all purpose flour
 2-½ cups sugar
 ½ cup vegetable oil
 4 eggs
 ½ t baking powder
 1 T baking soda
 2 t salt
 2 t cinnamon
 1 t cloves (ground)

Boil the raisins in the coffee (only a few minutes and let cool – or let sit over-night without boiling).
Stir together coffee, cherry juice, eggs, oil and baking soda.
Add all other ingredients and mix thoroughly so that all ingredients are evenly distributed.
Distribute between several small baking pans (3 or 4) and bake in a pre-heated 350 degree oven for a little over 1 hour or until an inserted toothpick comes out clean.

# Banana Fruit Cake

Use your favorite fruit cake recipe (or one of above) but add 2 mashed bananas for each loaf you bake.

# Brownies

**Ingredients:**
   4 squares of chocolate
   2 cups sugar
   1 cup shortening
   1 cup flour
   4 eggs
   2 cups nuts, chopped (your choice)
   2 t vanilla

Melt the chocolate and combine with the shortening. Beat the eggs well. Combine all ingredients. Bake for 25-30 minutes in a square or rectangular pan in a pre-heated 375 degree oven.

# Rhubarb Cake

**Ingredients:**
   2 cups rhubarb, cleaned, scraped and cut into ½ inch chunks
   2 eggs
   4 T butter, melted
   4 T sugar
   1-½ cups flour
   3 cups milk
   dash of salt

Sauté the rhubarb briefly in the melted butter. Spread evenly over the bottom of a greased baking dish. Meanwhile, combine all other ingredients into a batter. Pour the batter over the rhubarb. Bake in a medium oven. Serve with whipped cream topping or sprinkle with sugar while the cake is still hot.

# Butterscotch-Nut Cookies

**Ingredients for about 2 dozen cookies:**
   1 cup chopped nuts of your choosing (peanuts work just fine)
   1 pkg. butterscotch pudding mix
   ½ cup corn syrup
   4 cups corn flakes
   ½ stick butter (⅛ pound) sliced thin

Combine the butter chunks and syrup and heat and stir in a saucepan until butter melts.
Add the pudding mix and continue to heat and stir until it has boiled for a minute or two. Remove from heat and let cool 5 minutes, stirring the mixture at least twice during this time.
Add the nuts and corn flakes and stir until well blended.
Spoon onto wax paper or foil. Cool before serving.


# Cranberry-Nut Coffee Cake

**Ingredients:**
    2 cups Bisquick
    3 T sugar
    ½ can (1 cup) cranberry sauce
    2 eggs, beaten
    ⅔ cup milk

Combine all ingredients and pour into a 9 inch baking dish or pan.

**Ingredients for topping:**
    ⅔ cup chopped nuts of your choosing (walnuts or pecans work well)
    1 t cinnamon (ground)
    ½ cup brown sugar

Sprinkle over pan's contents.
Bake in a pre-heated 375 degree oven for 30 minutes or until an inserted toothpick comes out clean. Let cool and sprinkle with confectioner's sugar.

# Nutty Banana Cupcakes

**Ingredients for a dozen cupcakes:**
  ½ cup vegetable oil
  ½ stick butter (1/8 pound) softened
  1 cup sugar
  3 ripe bananas
  3 T milk
  2 eggs, beaten
  1 T vanilla extract
  1 T baking powder
  1 t baking soda
  dash of salt
  ½ cup chopped nuts of your choosing

Stir together the oil, butter and sugar.
Blend in the bananas, milk, eggs and vanilla.
Combine the remaining ingredients, then stir them thoroughly into the mixture.
Bake in a pre-heated 350 degree oven in paper-lined muffin cups* for 20 minutes or until an inserted toothpick comes out clean. Cool before serving.
*fill cups about 2/3 full


# Date-Nut Bread

**Ingredients:**
  ½ pound dates, pitted and chopped
  1 cup raisins
  1 cup chopped nuts of your choosing (walnuts work well)
  1 t baking soda
  1 cup water, boiling
  2 eggs, whites only
  2 cups all purpose flour
  1 cup sugar
  1 t baking powder

Combine nuts, dates and raisins. Sprinkle with baking soda and add boiling water.

Combine all other ingredients and add to the contents of the first bowl and mix thoroughly.

Bake in a greased loaf pan in a pre-heated 350 degree oven for 1 hour our until an inserted toothpick comes out clean.


## Banana Nut Bread with Fruit Ingredients

**Ingredients for 1 loaf:**
3 bananas, mashed
1 cup dried fruit, chopped (your choice, apricots, prunes, etc.)
1 cup chopped nuts (of your choosing)
½ cup citrus juice (lemon, lime or orange)
finely grated zest of whatever fruit you chose for juice
1 cup sugar
2 eggs
½ t baking soda
2 t baking powder
1-½ cups flour
½ pound butter (1 stick) melted
⅔ t salt

Combine flour, baking powder, baking soda and salt.
Blend together all other ingredients. Stir in flour mixture.
Spray 9x5 inch loaf-type pan with non-stick oil. Add dough. Bake in a pre-heated 350 degree oven for about 1 hour or until an inserted toothpick comes out clean.

# Apple Cake with Nuts

Ingredients:
  4 apples, peeled, cored and diced (about 2 cups)
  2 cups chopped nuts of your choosing, most any work well
  1 cup raisins (optional)
  2 cups all purpose flour
  4 eggs
  1-½ cups sugar
  1 T ground cinnamon
  1 cup vegetable oil
  1 t baking soda
  ½ t baking powder

Combine oil and sugar and beat until fluffy. Add eggs and beat thoroughly. Combine flour, cinnamon, baking powder and baking soda. Combine contents of the 2 bowls, and then blend in nuts, apples and raisins.
Pour into a lubricated cake pan. Bake in a 350 degree oven for 1 hour or until an inserted toothpick comes out clean.

# Fruit Pizza

Ingredients:
  1 pizza crust (medium size) baked
  6 T peach preserves
  4 apples, peeled, cored and diced (about 2 cups)
  1 cup raisins
  1 cup shredded or diced cheese (Monterey Jack works well)

Spread the peach preserves over the pizza crust. Scatter apples, raisins and cheese over pizza. Bake about 10 minutes or until cheese melts in a pre-heated 350 degree oven.

# Carrot Cake with Nuts

Ingredients:
   1 pkg. cake mix (about 20 oz.)
   2 cups shredded or finely chopped carrots
   1 cup chopped nuts of your choosing (pecans or walnuts work well)
   1-½ cups mayonnaise
   6 eggs
   2 T ground cinnamon
   ½ cup water

Combine and stir together cake mix, mayonnaise, eggs, cinnamon and water. Blend in carrots and nuts.
Bake in a lubricated cake pan in a pre-heated 350 degree oven for 45 minutes or until an inserted toothpick comes out clean.

Ingredients for frosting:
   1 pkg. cream cheese (12 oz.)
   ⅛ pound (½ stick) softened butter
   2 cups confectioners' sugar
   1 T vanilla extract
   4 T milk

Combine all 5 ingredients until spreading consistency is reached.

# Rice Krispie Bars

Ingredients:
   5 cups Rice Krispies
   4 cups miniature marshmallows
   ½ stick butter melted
   option: 1 cup peanut halves

Melt the butter and marshmallows together, stirring occasionally to blend. Remove from stove and add Rice Krispies. Stir until thoroughly coated. While still warm, press into a square pan. When cool, cut into squares.

# Banana Nut Raisin Bread

**Ingredients:**
- 2 cups all purpose flour
- 1 t baking powder
- ½ t baking soda
- 1 cup sugar
- ¼ t salt
- ½ stick butter (⅛ pound) melted
- 3 eggs
- 3 ripe bananas, mashed
- ½ cup milk
- 1 cup chopped nuts of your choosing (walnuts, peanuts or pecans work well)
- 1 cup raisins

Combine flour, baking soda, baking powder and salt. In a separate bowl, combine all other ingredients. Stir together the contents of both bowls.

Spoon into a lubricated loaf pan and bake in a pre-heated 350 degree oven for 1 hour or until an inserted toothpick comes out clean. Let cool before removing from pan.


# Chocolate Caramel Cake with Nuts

**Ingredients:**
- 1 box German chocolate cake mix
- 1 pound caramel candy
- 1 stick butter (¼ pound) diced
- 8 oz. chocolate chips
- 1 cup chopped nuts of your choice (walnuts or pecans work well)
- ⅓ cup milk

Prepare batter from directions on cake mix box. Pour half of it into a 13x9 inch lubricated pan and bake in a pre-heated 350 degree oven for 15 minutes.

Meanwhile, place the caramels, milk and melted butter in a saucepan over low heat. Stir until caramels melt.

Remove cake pan from oven and spoon the caramel mixture evenly over the cake. Scatter the nuts and chocolate chips on top and cover with the balance of the batter.

Return to the oven and continue baking 40 minutes longer or until an inserted toothpick comes out clean.

## Coconut-Cranberry-Orange Cake

**Ingredients:**
- 1 cup chopped cranberries (fresh or dry)
- ½ cup orange juice
- ⅔ cup toasted, chopped nuts of your choosing (walnuts or pecans work well)
- 3 T brown sugar
- 1 cup sugar
- 5 eggs
- 1-½ t vanilla extract
- 1 stick butter (¼ pound) softened
- 2 cups all purpose flour
- 1 t baking soda
- 1 t baking powder
- couple of "dashes" salt
- 2 cups sour cream
- 3 cups shredded or flaked coconut

Combine chopped cranberries and orange juice in a saucepan; heat and stir until juice is dissolved (or almost dissolved). Stir in nuts and brown sugar and set aside to cool.

Blend together the sugar and butter. Beat in one egg at a time. Stir in the vanilla extract. Stir in all remaining ingredients (not the orange-berry mixture). Blend thoroughly.

Spoon ⅓ of the mixture over the bottom of a cake pan. Spread ½ of the berry-juice mixture over the batter. Spoon another third of the batter over the berry mixture. Spread the rest of the berries over the batter. Spread the remainder of the batter on top.

Bake in a pre-heated 350 degree oven for about 1 hour or until an inserted toothpick comes out clean.

Serve as is or use an orange icing or dust with confectioner's sugar.


# Orange Flavored Pound Cake

**Ingredients:**
1-½ cups yellow cake mix
1 cup sugar (divided)
2 eggs
1 stick butter (¼ pound) softened
3 T grated orange zest
½ cup orange juice, divided
½ cup milk
½ t vanilla extract

Combine ½ of the sugar and the butter.

Beat in the eggs and orange zest (may want to use electric mixer).

Combine ½ the orange juice, milk and vanilla extract. Add to the egg-sugar mixture; also blend in the flour (cake mix).

Spoon batter into a lubricated loaf pan and bake in a pre-heated 350 degree oven for one hour our until an inserted toothpick comes out clean.

Meanwhile, stir together the remaining sugar and orange juice in a heated saucepan until the sugar melts. When the cake is done, spoon this over the cake.

# Apple-Nut Coffee Cake (a German recipe)

Ingredients:
  3-½ cups all purpose flour
  1 t salt
  ¾ cup sugar plus 1 T (divided)
  4 T milk
  2 sticks butter (½ pound)
  ½ cup warm water
  2 envelopes dry yeast
  4 eggs

Combine, in a large bowl that can be used with an electric mixer, ½ of the flour, 1 cup of sugar and the salt. Blend thoroughly.
Heat the milk and the butter in a saucepan until the butter is quite soft. Stir the dry yeast and 1 T sugar into the warm water. Yeast should foam. Add the yeast, milk and butter to the flour mixture and then blend in the eggs, one at a time, slowly. After 3 minutes, increase to medium speed for a couple of minutes until uniformly blended. Gradually, slowly, stir in the balance of the flour, a little at a time. Cover and let stand in a warm place about 30 minutes. Batter should nearly double in size.

Ingredients for frosting:
  1 cup chopped nuts (pecans or almonds work well)
  3 apples (4 if small) cored, peeled and sliced thin
  1 stick butter (¼ pound) melted
  1 t cinnamon
  ½ cup sugar

Combine ingredients and set aside until the dough has risen. When the dough has risen, knead it down, spoon the dough into a greased pan or baking dish and then spread frosting mixture on top. Cover and let stand 10 minutes. Meanwhile, pre-heat the oven to 350 degrees. After the 10 minutes, place in oven and let bake 50 minutes or until golden brown.

Ingredients for topping sauce:
  1 stick butter (¼ pound)
  1 cup sugar
  ½ cup light cream (half and half will work)
  1 t vanilla

Place ingredients in a saucepan and bring to a boil, stirring until butter is melted and ingredients are well blended.
Serve the topping sauce on the side with the coffee cake.

## Hazelnut Cookies

**Ingredients to make 4 dozen cookies:**
   1 stick (¼ pound) butter, softened
   2 cups chopped hazelnuts (may substitute nuts of your choosing, like almonds, pecans, or macadamia nuts)
   ½ cup sugar
   ⅔ cup brown sugar
   2 eggs
   2 cups all purpose flour
   1 t baking soda
   ½ t salt
   ⅔ t vanilla extract
   2 heaping cups chocolate chips

Blend both sugars, eggs, vanilla and butter (about 2 minutes).
Combine flour, baking soda and salt. Add to the sugar-butter mixture and blend. Stir in the chopped nuts and chocolate chips. Cover and refrigerate several hours.
Drop 1 tablespoon full at a time on a baking sheet and bake in a preheated 350 degree oven for 15 minutes or until a golden brown.

# Pineapple Carrot Cake with Chopped Nuts

**Ingredients:**
  1-½ cups chopped nuts of your choosing (pecans work well)
  2 cups all purpose flour
  2 cups grated carrots
  1-½ cups brown sugar
  2 t baking soda
  1 t salt
  2 T lemon juice
  ¾ cup vegetable oil
  1 t vanilla extract
  1 – 20 oz. can crushed pineapple (save the juice)
  vegetable oil spray to lubricate the pan/dish

Combine nuts, flour, carrots, brown sugar, baking soda and salt.
Combine the lemon juice, vegetable oil, vanilla and pineapple juice
and stir into the mixture of dry ingredients.
Stir in the pineapple.
Bake in a greased 13x9 inch (or the equivalent) baking dish or pan
and bake in a pre-heated 350 degree oven for 45 minutes or until an
inserted toothpick comes out clean.

**Ingredients for the frosting:**
  1 – 8 oz. pkg. cream cheese
  3 T sugar (preferably confectioners')
  whipped cream (at least twice the volume of the cheese)

Beat the cream cheese and sugar until smooth, and then blend in the
whipped cream.

# Almond Cake

**Ingredients:**
- 1 cup almonds – chopped fine in a blender
- ½ cup sugar
- 3 eggs
- 1 stick butter (¼ pound) softened
- 1 T vanilla extract
- ½ t almond extract
- 1-½ cups cake flour (or all purpose)
- 1 t baking powder
- 3 T powdered sugar for topping
- vegetable oil spray to lubricate pan or dish

Blend butter and sugar together. Blend in chopped almonds. Stir in one egg at a time. Slowly stir in flour and remaining ingredients (except powdered sugar). If the batter seems to dry, add a little milk. Fold the batter into an 8x8 (or thereabouts) greased baking pan or dish. Bake in a pre-heated 350 degree oven for 45 minutes or until an inserted toothpick comes out clean.
Dust surface with powdered sugar.

# Macaroon (anise flavored finger-shaped cookies)*

**Ingredients for "one batch":**
- 4-½ cups flour
- ⅓ cup sugar
- 1 t salt
- 1 cup vegetable oil
- ¾ cup water
- 2 t ground anise seed
- 3 t baking powder
- 1 pound walnuts cut lengthwise

Sift dry ingredients into a large bowl. Heat oil until hot, then pour over dry ingredients and mix with a large spoon. When cool enough, mix with hands like a pie crust. Add ¾ cup of water and continue mixing. Cover and set aside for 15 minutes.

Take a small piece of dough (size of walnut) and roll out in a thin circle. Put pieces of walnuts in a line in the dough and roll dough in the shape of a cigar. Lay side by side on a cookie sheet and bake at 300 degrees for about 30 minutes (on the bottom rack for 10 minutes and on the top rack for 20 minutes or until golden brown.)

**Then dip them in a basic syrup called "Ather":**
   3 cups sugar
   1-½ cups water
   1 T orange blossom water or rosewater

Mix ingredients well before heating. Heat to a boil, and then simmer for 20 minutes.

*Courtesy Judy Droubie, Staples, MN


# Rhubarb Crunch*

**Ingredients to serve 4 or 5:**
   4 cups rhubarb, chopped
   1 cup sugar
   2 T flour
   butter

Mix together first 3 ingredients and pour into a 9x9 inch pan. Dot with butter.

**Next:**
   1 cup sugar
   1 cup flour
   1 t baking powder
   ¼ t salt
   1 large egg, beaten

Mix together dry ingredients and stir in the egg. Mixture will be crumbly. Pour over rhubarb mixture in pan and shake to settle. Bake 45 minutes in a 350 degree oven or till light brown.
Serve with ice cream or whipped cream.

*Courtesy Helen Mennis, Staples, MN

# Crumbly Fruit Pie

**Ingredients:**
    14 graham cracker squares – crushed fine
    1-½ t cinnamon
    1 stick (¼ pound) butter, divided and melted
    5-½ cups thinly sliced apples or other fruit of your choosing
    1 cup all purpose flour, divided
    ¾ cup sugar
    1 t vanilla extract
    ½ cup brown sugar

Combine ½ t cinnamon, graham cracker crumbs and half the melted butter. Press onto the bottom and sides of a 9 inch pie plate.
For the filling, combine the sliced apples, white sugar, vanilla and ¼ cup of flour. Spoon into the crust.
For the top, combine ¾ cup of flour, 1 t cinnamon and the brown sugar. Then blend in the remainder of the melted butter until the mixture looks "crumbly". Sprinkle the mixture over the filling.
Bake in a pre-heated 350 degree oven for 1 hour. Filling should be soft and bubbly.

# Fresh Raspberry Pie

**Ingredients:**
  1 – 9 inch pastry shell, baked
  5 cups fresh raspberries – divided
  2 T lemon juice
  1 cup sugar
  3 T cornstarch
  1 cup water – divided
  4 oz. cream cheese
  1 T butter – melted
  1 T milk


Combine 1 cup of raspberries and ⅔ cup of water in a saucepan and simmer 4 minutes. Strain out the seeds and set the juice aside.
In a different saucepan, combine the sugar, cornstarch and the rest of the water; stir until smooth. Add the raspberry juice; cook and stir a couple of minutes until it starts to thicken.
Stir in the lemon juice and let cool.
Combine the butter, cream cheese and milk and beat until smooth. Spread this mixture over the bottom and along the sides of the baked pastry shell. Fill the pie shell with the rest of the berries and sprinkle the sugar-water-cornstarch-lemon juice combination evenly over the berries.
Refrigerate before serving.

# Mincemeat Pie

Ingredients:
   Pie crust dough for top and bottom for 9 inch pie tin or plate
   1 pear, peeled, cored and diced
   3 apples, (hard) peeled, cored and diced
   ⅔ cup raisins
   1 cup dates, pitted and chopped
   2 T grated orange peel
   ⅓ cup orange juice
   1 cup brown sugar
   ½ cup brandy
   1 T cinnamon
   1 t allspice (ground)
   1 t cloves (ground)
   ½ stick butter, diced

Roll out dough for bottom of pan (about 13 inch diameter for a 9 inch tin). Fit into pie tin; trim edges.
Combine all ingredients except butter and spoon into pie tin. Sprinkle diced butter over all.
Cover with dough for top crust. Prick several places with fork. Flute edges. Option: brush with melted butter and sprinkle with granulated sugar.
Bake in a pre-heated 375 degree oven for 1 hour. If crust edges start to brown ahead of the rest of the crust, cover with foil.

# Peach Pie

Ingredients for 9 inch pie:
   Pastry for double crust
   8 cups sliced peaches (peeled)
   1 t ground cinnamon
   ½ t nutmeg, ground
   ½ t ginger, ground
   1 cup sugar (plus 2 Ts)
   3 T cornstarch
   1 T lemon juice
   ½ cup heavy cream (divided)

Roll out the dough for the crust and line pie tin or plate.
Combine all dry ingredients in a bowl and then stir in the lemon juice
and half the cream.
Add the sliced peaches and gently stir together. Pour into the pie plate.
Roll out the rest of the pastry and cover, fluting the edges. Brush on the
rest of the cream and sprinkle with the rest of the sugar. Pierce the
crust several places with a fork. Bake in a pre-heated 375 degree oven
for 1 hour.
Cool before serving.

## Pecan Pie

### Ingredients:
  1 unbaked pie crust
  1 cup corn syrup (white)
  ½ stick butter (⅛ pound) melted
  ⅔ cup sugar
  4 eggs
  1 t vanilla extract
  1 T all purpose flour
  2 T sugar
  dash salt
  1-½ cups halved pecans

Combine the melted butter, corn syrup and sugar in a saucepan and
bring to a boil for 1 minute. Beat eggs and combine with syrup mixture. Stir in vanilla extract.
Place pie crust on bottom of pie plate or tin. Combine flour and 2 T
sugar and sprinkle over pie crust. Pour in the filling and top with
pecan halves. Bake in a pre-heated 400 degree oven for 10 minutes.
Cool before serving.

## Rhubarb Pie

### Ingredients:
  4 cups chopped rhubarb
  1-½ cups sugar
  3 eggs, beaten
  ¼ cup flour
  ¾ t nutmeg
  options – substitute 1 cup strawberries for 1 cup rhubarb

Using the same procedure as for any two-crusted pie, combine the dry ingredients; stir the beaten eggs in (thoroughly); stir in the rhubarb and place mixture, evenly, in the pie crust shell. Cover with top crust.

**Ingredients for topping:**
½ cup flour
½ cup sugar
½ cup butter

Combine the flour and sugar. Cut the butter into small pieces and stir into the dry mixture. Sprinkle topping over crust. Cover with foil and bake in a pre-heated 400 degree oven for 20 minutes. Remove foil and bake another 20 minutes or until crust is a golden brown.

## Blueberry Pie

**Ingredients:**
3 cups cleaned berries, remove all unripe berries
1 cup sugar (rounded)
3 T flour
2 T butter, melted
dash of salt

Using the same procedure as for any two-crust pie, bake in a pre-heated 350 degree oven for 45 minutes. Sprinkle sugar over top crust.

## Lemon Pie

**Ingredients for 1 pie:**
1 – 9 inch pastry shell, baked

**Filling ingredients:**
½ cup freshly squeezed lemon juice
1 cup sugar
2-½ cups milk
4 egg yolks, beaten
½ cup all purpose flour
3 T butter

**Meringue ingredients:**
  Whites of four eggs
  ½ cup sugar

Stir together flour, sugar and milk until smooth. Heat, in a saucepan until it starts to thicken. If it starts to boil, reduce heat and continue stirring and cooking a couple of minutes more. Slowly add and stir in the beaten egg yolks and continue to heat for a couple minutes longer. Remove from heat and add lemon juice and flakes of butter. Stir until butter melts. Keep on low heat.

Combine the sugar with the egg whites and beat until peaks form.

Pour the filling into the pastry shell. Spread the meringue over the filling and bake in a pre-heated 350 degree oven until meringue starts to turn brown.

Remove from oven and let cool (about an hour). Refrigerate leftovers.

# CHAPTER XII

# DESSERTS

# Strawberry-Lime Parfait

**Ingredients to serve 4:**
   1 pkg. frozen strawberries, thawed*
   1 lime, quartered
   ⅔ cup whipped cream

Combine whipped cream with strawberries in 4 parfait glasses. Invite guests to squeeze lime juice over contents.
*Fresh strawberries may be used, but they should be halved and the whipped cream sweetened with 2 T sugar.


# Blueberry-Kiwi Parfait

**Ingredients to serve 4:**
   2 cups blueberries, either fresh or frozen-thawed
   2 kiwis, peeled and diced
   ⅔ cup whipped cream
   2 T sugar
   1 t cinnamon

Blend the sugar and cinnamon into the whipped cream.
Stir the fruit into the whipped cream. Serve in parfait glasses.


# Raspberry Parfait

**Ingredients to serve 6:**
   4 cups raspberries (save out 6 large raspberries to top desserts)
   2 sticks cinnamon
   2 cups sugar
   3 cups water
   2 T cornstarch
   whipped cream

Place the raspberries, cinnamon, sugar and water in a saucepan and bring to a boil, then reduce heat and stir for 5 minutes.
Cool, and then strain through a sieve.
Re-heat the berry juice, adding a little cornstarch at a time to thicken.
Place in parfait glasses and top with whipped cream and a berry.

# Peaches and Cream

**Ingredients for 1 pie:**
1 – 9 inch pastry shell, baked or make a graham cracker crust
(crushed crackers with 1 stick (½ pound) softened butter
20 full size marshmallows
2 cups milk
6 large or 8 small fresh peaches, pitted, peeled and sliced
1-½ cups whipped cream

Place the marshmallows and milk in a saucepan and melt the marsh-mallows over low heat. Pour off excess milk.
Fold in peach slices and whipped cream and ladle into the pie shell (in a pie tin). Refrigerate at least 2 hours.

# Simply Scrumptillyicious!

**Ingredients to serve 4:**
2 bananas, sliced
sections of 2 oranges or 3 tangerines or 4 clementines
1 apple, cored and sliced thin
2 kiwis, sliced
1 cup seedless grapes (halved if you have the time)
1 cup almonds (preferably slivered)
2 cups of bite-size angel food cake
1 cup sliced strawberries (frozen or fresh)
1 cup orange juice
whipped cream

Serve in large sherbet type glasses.
Mix the fruit (except the strawberries) nuts and cake pieces and distribute equally in the dessert dishes. Drizzle the orange juice over the fruit in each dish. Top with whipped cream and garnish with the strawberries.

# Wild Rice with Granola

Ingredients:
  2 cups cooked wild rice
  1 cup granola
  ¼ cup dates, chopped
  ¼ cup chopped nuts
  ½ cup brown sugar
  1 small bottle maraschino cherries, chopped
  whipped cream for topping

Prepare the wild rice by covering ¾ cup rice with 2-½ cups water. Bring to a boil and then reduce heat, cover and let simmer 1-½ hours until well "flowered".
Combine all ingredients. Serve hot or cold in dishes. Top with whipped cream and a cherry.

# Wild Rice with Fruit

  2 cups cooked wild rice, chilled (see previous recipe for cooking instructions)
  1 - #2 can fruit cocktail
  1 small can crushed pineapple
  1 cup miniature marshmallows
  2 cups whipped cream

Combine all ingredients and either stir in or top with whipped cream and a cherry.

# Apple Cobbler

**Ingredients:**
6 hard apples, peeled, cored and sliced or diced
1 cup brown sugar
1 t ground cloves
2 t cinnamon
1-½ cups all purpose flour
½ stick (⅛ pound) butter, diced
3 T vegetable oil
1 t baking powder
½ t baking soda
dash of salt
2 cup yogurt (apple flavor if available, otherwise plain)
1 cup chopped pecans or nuts of your choosing
ice cream

In a pan or oven proof dish, combine the apples, brown sugar, cloves, cinnamon and 4 T of flour. Scatter diced pieces of butter over-all.
In a separate bowl combine the rest of the flour, baking powder, baking soda, salt and oil and then add and stir in the yogurt. Spoon over the apple mixture.
Scatter the nuts on top.
Bake in a pre-heated 375 degree oven for 30 minutes or until it has turned a golden brown.
Serve with ice cream.


# Apple Streusel

**Ingredients to serve 12:**
1-½ cups sugar
½ cup shortening
½ cup butter
3 cups all purpose flour
4 eggs
½ t baking powder
1 t almond extract
1 t vanilla
8 medium apples, peeled, cored and sliced thin

Soften butter. Combine butter, sugar and shortening.

Add eggs and extracts and blend until uniform color.

Stir baking powder into flour and stir into the above ingredients.

Spread batter at a uniform thickness in a baking dish (approximately 10x15 inches)

Scatter apple slices on top of batter.

**Prepare a topping from the following:**
   ½ cup chopped walnuts or pecans
   ⅓ cups all purpose flour
   ⅓ cup brown sugar
   4 T butter, melted

Combine all 4 ingredients and spread over apples.

Dissolve 1 cup confectioner's sugar in 1 cup milk and sprinkle over apples.

Bake in a pre-heated 350 degree oven for 45 minutes or until glaze is a golden brown.


# Apple Cake

**Ingredients:**
   Peel, core and chop enough hard apples to equal 3 cups
   1-½ cups sugar
   1 T vanilla extract
   ½ cup vegetable oil
   3 eggs
   3 cups all purpose flour
   1 t baking soda
   1 T baking powder
   3 t cinnamon
   ½ cup frozen lemonade concentrate (thawed)
   vegetable oil spray to prepare baking pan or oven-proof dish, about 10x12 inches

Using a mixer, beat eggs thoroughly, add sugar and mix again.
In another bowl, combine dry ingredients. Add to egg-sugar mixture and blend again.
Add lemonade concentrate, vegetable oil and vanilla extract and blend again.
Add chopped apples and stir together once more.
Pour batter into a pan you have sprayed with vegetable oil. Bake in a pre-heated 350 degree oven for about an hour or until an inserted toothpick comes out clean.

# Apple-Pecan Bars

**Ingredients:**
½ cup pecans that have been toasted and chopped
2 cups chopped apples that have been peeled and cored
1 stick melted butter
1 cup all purpose flour
1 cup sugar
1 egg
1 t baking soda
1 t baking powder
2 t cinnamon
¼ t salt

Beat together the egg, butter and sugar. Add the chopped apples and pecans. Work in the remaining ingredients. Bake in an 8x10 pan or oven-proof dish (that has been sprayed with vegetable oil) in a pre-heated 350 degree oven for 45 minutes.
Let cool and cut into bars.

# Apple Crisp

**Ingredients to serve 6:**
  8 hard, crisp apples, peeled, cored and sliced thin
  1-½ cups all purpose flour
  1-½ cups regular (not quick) oatmeal
  2 cups chopped nuts (walnuts or pecans work well)
  2 t cinnamon
  1 cup brown sugar (heaping)
  ½ cup sugar
  ½ t salt
  1 stick butter (¼ pound) diced and melted
  4 T lemon juice
  whipped cream

Toss apple slices with lemon juice and sugar (granulated).
Combine flour, oatmeal, nuts, cinnamon, brown sugar, salt and melted butter.
Place apple slices in bottom of a lubricated baking dish and cover with oatmeal mixture.
Bake in a pre-heated 350 degree oven for 1 hour or until topping is a golden brown. Let cool and serve with whipped cream.

# Stuffed Apples #1

**Ingredients to serve 4:**
  4 apples, cored
  4 T brown sugar
  4 t cinnamon
  4 T butter, melted

Combine the sugar, cinnamon and melted butter and stuff each apple. Place in an oven proof dish and bake 20 minutes in a 350 degree oven or until tender.

# Stuffed Apples #2

**Ingredients to serve 4:**
  4 large apples (preferably a hard variety) peeled and cored.
  your favorite jam
  3 eggs, separated
  3 T sugar
  2 T ground nuts (of your choice)

Peel and core the apples. Stuff them with the jam. Beat the egg yolks and sugar together. Beat the whites until still and add to the yolks. Pour over apples and then sprinkle each apple with the ground nuts. Bake in a 400 degree oven for about 20 minutes.


# Stuffed Apples #3

**Ingredients to serve 4:**
  4 large hard baking apples, cored
  1 cup chopped nuts of your choosing, like walnuts or pecans
  4 T brown sugar
  4 T melted butter

Core the apples. Toast the nuts in a Teflon pan about 2 minutes over medium heat, stirring occasionally. Combine the nuts, brown sugar and butter and stuff the apples. Place the stuffed apples in a baking dish in about an inch of water.
Bake about 45 minutes in a pre-heated 370 degree oven. Spoon the liquid over the apples 2 or 3 times during the baking time.


# Stuffed Apples #4

**Ingredients to stuff 6 apples:**
  6 hard apples, cores removed
  ½ cup chopped nuts (like pecans or almonds)
  ½ cup raisins
  ½ cup brown sugar
  ⅓ cup chopped cranberries (cooked or raw)
  1 t cinnamon, ground
  2 T melted butter

Combine all stuffing ingredients and stuff centers of apples. There will be stuffing left over; mound this on top of each apple.

Place apples in a baking dish or pan. Add 1-½ cups water to dish. Bake in a pre-heated 350 degree oven for 45 minutes or until apples are soft.

## Apple Brown Betty

**Ingredients to serve 8:**
  8 hard apples, peeled, cored and sliced
  1 cup prunes, pitted and chopped (coarse)
  4 T lemon or lime juice
  3 cups bread crumbs (crumble bread at least 1 day old)
  1 stick (¼ pound) butter, melted
  1 cup brown sugar
  1 T ground cinnamon
  dash or 2 of salt

Place apple slices, chopped prunes and lemon juice in a large bowl and toss until fruit is coated.

Combine sugar, cinnamon and salt.

Toss together melted butter and bread crumbs.

Scatter a third of the bread crumbs over the bottom of a 9x12 (or thereabouts) baking dish or pan. Cover crumbs with half of the fruit mixture. Sprinkle with half the sugar-cinnamon-salt mixture. Sprinkle with another third of the crumbs. Cover with the other half of the fruit. Sprinkle with remaining sugar mixture and top it all off with the remainder of the crumbs.

Bake in a pre-heated 400 degree oven, covered with foil, for about 45 minutes. Remove foil and continue to bake until crumbs are a golden brown.

# Brown Betty Blueberry Crisp

**Ingredients to serve 4:**
  4 cups blueberries (fresh or frozen)
  2 T cornstarch
  1 T lemon juice
  ⅓ cup water
  4 T sugar
  1-½ cups instant oatmeal
  ½ cup brown sugar
  ½ cup all purpose flour
  1 T cinnamon
  ½ stick (⅛ pound) butter
  4 scoops ice cream

Combine cornstarch, lemon juice, water and sugar and stir until dry ingredients dissolve.
Cover bottom of oven-proof, lubricated baking dish with berries. Pour above liquid over berries.
Combine oatmeal, flour, brown sugar and cinnamon and put on top of berries, flake chips of butter at random over all.
Bake in a pre-heated 350 degree oven for 25 minutes.
Serve along side vanilla ice cream.


# Pears and Raspberries or Blueberries

**Ingredients to serve 4:**
  4 large ripe pears, cored, peeled and halved
  2 cups berries
  ½ cup sugar
  2 cups grape juice (preferably white)
  whipped cream

Puree berries, grape juice and sugar briefly, until well blended. Place 2 pear halves on each plate and pour juices over them. Top with whipped cream.

# Glorified Rice

Ingredients:
  3 cups cooked rice
  1 cup whipped cream, sweetened
  1 can fruit cocktail, medium (#2)
  1 small can crushed pineapple
  1 small jar maraschino cherries
  1 cup miniature marshmallows

Drain the cans and jar. Combine all ingredients and chill before serving.

# Glorified Wild Rice

Ingredients:
  2 cups wild rice, cooked
  2 pkgs. strawberry Jell-O
  4 cups hot water
  1 medium can crushed pineapple
  2 cups whipped cream (or substitute)
  1 cup marshmallow bits

Prepare Jell-O and set until it thickens.
Beat whipped cream and Jell-O together; stir in remaining ingredients.
Chill before serving.
Additional whipped cream may be used as a topping.

# Hot Plum Sauce

Ingredients to serve 4:
  24 plums, halved
  ½ cup maple syrup
  ½ cup honey
  2 cups water
  6 whole allspice
  1 stick cinnamon, broken into 4 pieces

While the oven is warming to 350 degrees, combine in a saucepan, all ingredients, except the plums, and bring to a boil.

Arrange the half-plums in a flat baking dish and pour the liquid and spices over all. Cover the dish (you may use foil) and bake 45 minutes. Let cook briefly but serve hot in sauce dishes.

# Strawberry-Rhubarb Dessert

**Ingredients for 6 servings:**
  4 cups chopped rhubarb
  3 cups strawberry halves
  2 cups sugar
  ½ stick (⅛ pound) butter

**Crust ingredients:**
  ⅔ cup oil
  2 cups all purpose flour
  2 T sugar
  dash or 2 or salt
  ½ cup warm milk
  ice cream

Combine the rhubarb, strawberries and sugar and cover the bottom of a pan or oven-safe baking dish (about 6x12).

Make a crust by combining the flour, sugar, oil and half the milk. Stir ingredients together until they form a doughy ball. Place the ball between
2 sheets of foil or wax paper and using a rolling pin, flatten until it is the approximate size of the pan. Peel off the top foil or wax paper, then turn it over onto the pan – dough side down; then peel off the other foil or wax paper. Brush the dough with the other half of the milk and sprinkle with the sugar.

Bake in a pre-heated 375 degree oven for about 1 hour or until a golden brown.

Serve with ice cream.

# Cantaloupe Cradle

**Ingredients:**
Prepare a half a cantaloupe for each person by scraping out the seeds.
Fill the hollow of each with:
Grapes
Banana slices
Strawberries

Sprinkle contents with 2 T maple syrup per half cantaloupe. Salad
dressing recipes found in Chapter I also work well.

# Poached Pears

**Ingredients:**
2 medium size pears per serving

**Ingredients for poaching liquid:**
4 cups white wine
3 cups water
1-½ cups sugar
2 – 3 inch sticks of cinnamon

Peel the pears but leave stems. Slice a little off the bottom of each pear
so they will sit upright in the saucepan.
Place the liquid ingredients in a saucepan that is just wide enough in
diameter to hold the number of pears you wish to poach. Bring the
liquid to a boil, stirring until the sugar dissolves. Add the pears and
reduce heat to simmer. Let simmer (hot but not boiling) 20 minutes.
Serve pears hot or cold, with or without liquid.

# Angel Food Dessert with Cherries

Ingredients:
  1 angel food cake
  2 cups whipped cream (sweetened)
  3 cups milk
  4 egg yolks
  1 cup sugar
  2 T gelatin (unflavored)
  4 egg whites, beaten
  ½ cup water
  1 small jar maraschino cherries

Place the milk in a saucepan. Stir in salt. Stir in the egg yolks, thoroughly. Add sugar and bring to a boil. Add the gelatin to the half-cup of water and stir into the milk-egg mixture. Let cool.
Stir in beaten egg whites. Let stand until the mixture begins to "set". Fold in the whipped cream. Cut or tear the angel food cake into small pieces. Layer the cake pieces on the bottom of a 9x13 pan. Pour the liquid uniformly over the cake pieces. Cut up the cherries and scatter over the dessert.


# Pecan Caramel Treats

Ingredients to serve 6:
  Pie crust dough or pre-made crust
  1 cup heavy cream
  1-½ cups sugar
  1 stick butter, shaved
  2 cups pecans, toasted
  1 t vanilla
  dash of salt

Line a pie tine with pie crust dough. Bake in a pre-heated 350 degree oven until a golden brown. Remove from oven and let cool.
Meanwhile, heat the sugar in a saucepan until it caramelizes. Carefully stir in the cream. Cook over low heat until the caramel is dissolved. Remove from heat and stir in the remaining ingredients until they are evenly distributed.
Spread the mixture over the pie crust and return to the oven. Let heat 20 minutes or until it bubbles.
Let cool and then cut into wedges or squares.

# Almond Balls

**Ingredients for about 2 dozen balls:**
   1-½ cups finely chopped almonds (toasted first)
   1-½ cups chocolate chips (either white or dark)
   ½ cup cream (heavy)
   2 T almond liqueur
   confectioners' sugar

Toast the almonds in a pre-heated 350 degree oven for a couple of minutes. Chop very fine.
Using a double boiler, melt the chocolate chips in the cream. Stir in the chopped almonds and the almond liqueur.
Refrigerate (at least a couple of hours) until the substance can be formed into balls, using a spoon and your fingers (dust your fingers first with confectioners' sugar).
Roll the balls in the sugar and refrigerate until ready to serve.

# Pecan Bars

**Ingredients for 2 dozen bars:**
   ¾ cup sugar
   ¾ cup maple flavored syrup
   3 eggs
   ⅛ pound (½ stick) butter, melted
   1 t vanilla extract
   1 cup chocolate chips, semi sweet
   1-½ cups chopped pecans, not too fine

**Use "store-bought" pie crust or use this recipe:**
   1-⅔ cups all purpose flour
   ¼ pound (1 stick) butter, melted
   ½ cup brown sugar

Combine crust ingredients, beating until crumbly. Press onto the bottom of a lightly greased pan or baking dish. Bake for 15 minutes in a pre-heated 350 degree oven (or until brown).
Beat eggs and then combine, thoroughly, with remaining ingredients. Spoon evenly over crust and bake 30 minutes in the 350 degree oven. Cut into serving size bars.

# Crumbly Peach Dessert

**Ingredients to serve 4:**
  6 peaches, peeled and pitted and diced
  1-½ cups pecan or almond cookie crumbs (off the grocer's shelf)
  1 cup sugar
  1-½ cups whipping cream

Using a rolling pin and wax paper or foil, roll the cookies into fine crumbs.
Whip the cream and combine with peaches, sugar and crumbs.
Refrigerate (or freeze) before serving.


# Maple Nut Sundae

**Ingredients to serve 4:**
  4 large or 8 small scoops vanilla ice cream
  ½ cup maple syrup
  ⅓ cup chunky peanut butter
  ⅔ cup cashew halves

Beat together the syrup and peanut butter. Pour over servings of ice cream. Scatter cashew halves over each serving.


# Lemon Yogurt

**Ingredients to serve 4:**
  1 carton unflavored yogurt (32 oz.)
  ½ cup fresh squeezed lemon juice
  2 cups sugar

Combine all 3 ingredients and either refrigerate or freeze. Other fruit flavors will also work well, such as strawberry, raspberry or blueberry, either using just the juice or juice and the berries.

# Apple Topping for Ice Cream

4 apples, peeled, cored and sliced
cooking oil
4 T sugar
3 T cinnamon

Fry the apple slices in the cooking oil until tender.
Combine the sugar and cinnamon and sprinkle over apple slices.
Serve over ice cream.

# Chocolate-Almond Candy

**Ingredients for 2 dozen pieces of candy:**
1 cup almonds, toasted and chopped fine
1-½ cups chocolate chips*
½ cup whipping cream
1 T almond liqueur
½ cup confectioners' sugar

Using a double boiler, melt the chocolate chips in the cream.
Meanwhile, toast the almonds 2 or 3 minutes in a non-stick pan, stirring occasionally. Let cool and chop fine.
Stir the almonds and liqueur into the chocolate-cream mixture.
Refrigerate until it is thick enough to roll into balls (a couple of hours).
Spread the sugar over a flat surface. Dust fingers with the sugar. Roll into balls and roll balls in the sugar. Refrigerate in a shallow, flat pan until served.
*may use white chocolate chips

# Nutty Fruit Dessert

**Ingredients to serve 6:**
⅓ cup sour cream
½ cup cottage cheese
4 T honey
½ t almond extract
3 cups mixed fresh fruit (like raspberries, strawberries, blueberries, etc.)
½ cup sliced almonds or cashew halves

Prepare the cottage cheese ahead of time by blending it (in a blender) until smooth. Refrigerate several hours (6-8) until smooth.

Stir the sour cream, honey and almond extract into the cottage cheese. If you use strawberries, slice them. Gently stir all the fruit together and divide equally among the 6 dessert dishes (parfait glasses work well). Top each serving of fruit with the cottage cheese mixture and sprinkle with nuts.

## Banana Pudding

**Ingredients:**
  3 ripe bananas, sliced and divided
  1-⅓ cups vanilla wafers, crushed into crumbs and divided
  1 pkg. vanilla pudding mix
  1 pkg. strawberry, raspberry or lemon gelatin
  whipped cream
  vegetable oil spray

Spread ½ of the wafer crumbs over the bottom of a 10 inch square pan, pre-sprayed with vegetable oil.

Prepare the vanilla pudding mix and spoon over the crumbs while still hot.

Spread a little less than half the banana slices over the pudding.

Top with the remaining wafer crumbs. Refrigerate at least 1 hour.

Prepare the gelatin and let cool until it starts to set, then pour over the crumbs.

Layer most of the remaining banana slices over the gelatin, saving enough to garnish each serving with a slice.

Cover with a generous layer of whipped cream and garnish with remaining banana slices.

# Banana-Pineapple Dessert

**Ingredients to serve 8:**
  2 cups crushed graham crackers
  2 sticks (½ pound) butter, softened and divided
  3 bananas, sliced
  2 small cans crushed or diced pineapple, drained
  2 eggs
  2 cups powdered sugar
  3 cups whipped cream
  1 t vanilla
  1 cup chopped nuts of your choosing

Prepare a crust by thoroughly mixing the cracker crumbs and 1 stick softened butter. Cover the bottom of a baking dish or pan approximately 9x12 in size. Press down with a large spoon or similar instrument. Bake in a pre-heated 350 degree oven for 15 minutes. Let cool. Combine rest of butter, sugar, eggs and vanilla with an electric mixer, thoroughly. Spread this mixture evenly over the cracker crumb crust. Scatter banana slices over mixture. Spread pineapple over bananas. Cover with a liberal amount of whipped cream. Sprinkle chopped nuts over all.
Option: drain and chop up a small jar of maraschino cherries and scatter over all.

# Spiced Peaches or Pears

**Ingredients to serve 4:**
  4 peaches or pears, peeled and cut in half
  ½ cup water
  ½ cup sugar
  8 cloves
  1 cinnamon stick
  ¼ cup vinegar
  brown sugar and sour cream for use when served

Place the water, sugar, cloves, cinnamon and vinegar in a saucepan. Stir together, then bring to a boil and then reduce heat and simmer for 10 minutes. Add the fruit and simmer another 10 minutes.

Discard the cinnamon stick. Place the fruit in a flat baking dish or pan and pour liquid over all. Cover and refrigerate (serve cold).

Serve fruit in sauce dishes (2 halves per serving) and top with a dollop of sour cream and sprinkle with brown sugar.

## Banana Karma*

**Ingredients to serve 4:**
  4 bananas, peeled and sliced
  1 cup sour cream
  1 cup mayonnaise
  2 t vanilla extract
  4 T sugar

Combine all but sugar in a shallow, oven-safe dish. Sprinkle surface with sugar. Broil until sugar melts (not caramelized).

*Courtesy Greg Johnson, St. Cloud, MN

# Other Books by Duane R. Lund

A Beginner's Guide to Hunting and Trapping
A Kid's Guidebook to Fishing Secrets
Fishing and Hunting Stories from The Lake of the Woods
Andrew, Youngest Lumberjack
The Youngest Voyageur
White Indian Boy
Gull Lake, Yesterday and Today
Lake of the Woods, Yesterday and Today, Vol. 1
Lake of the Woods, Earliest Accounts, Vol. 2
Lake of the Woods (The Last 50 Years and the Next)
Leech Lake, Yesterday and Today
The North Shore of Lake Superior, Yesterday and Today
Our Historic Boundary Waters
Our Historic Upper Mississippi
Tales of Four Lakes and a River
The Indian Wars
Chief Flatmouth
101 Favorite Freshwater Fish Recipes
101 Favorite Wild Rice Recipes
101 Favorite Mushroom Recipes
150 Ways to Enjoy Potatoes
Early Native American Recipes and Remedies
Camp Cooking, Made Easy and Fun
Cooking Minnesotan, yoo-betcha!
more than 50 Ways to enjoy Lefse
Entertainment Helpers, Quick and Easy
Gourmet Freshwater Fish Recipes
Nature's Bounty for Your Table
Sauces, Seasonings and Marinades for Fish and Wild Game
The Scandinavian Cookbook
The Soup Cookbook
Traditional Holiday Ethnic Recipes - collected all over the world
The Life And Times of THREE POWERFUL OJIBWA CHIEFS,
*Curly Head Hole-In-The-Day the elder, Hole-In-The-Day the younger*
Hasty But Tasty
Europeans In North America *Before Columbus*

## About the Author

- EDUCATOR (RETIRED, SUPERINTENDENT OF SCHOOLS, STAPLES, MINNESOTA);
- HISTORIAN (PAST MEMBER OF EXECUTIVE BOARD, MINNESOTA HISTORICAL SOCIETY);
  Past Member of BWCA and National Wilderness Trails Advisory Committees;
- SENIOR CONSULTANT to the Blandin Foundation
- WILDLIFE ARTIST, OUTDOORSMAN.